THE VIETNAM WAR

Globe Fearon Educational Publisher
A Division of Simon & Schuster
Upper Saddle River, New Jersey

About the Reviewers

Burton F. Beers is Professor of History at North Carolina State University. He has taught American foreign relations and Asian history and has published numerous scholarly articles and books on United States relations with East Asia. He is co-author of a widely used college text, *The Far East,* and senior author of a best-selling high school text, *World History: Patterns of Civilization.* Dr. Beers is currently directing the production of a series of fourth through seventh grade social studies textbooks to be published by North Carolina State University for the North Carolina Schools.

Rose Ann Mulford is a high school social studies teacher in the Livingston, New Jersey, Public Schools. She received a Bachelor of Arts degree in elementary education at Trenton State College and a Masters degree in Educational Psychology at Montclair State University. Mrs. Mulford has completed graduate work in Constitutional Law and Government at Rutgers University. In addition to United States history, Mrs. Mulford has taught Holocaust, American government, psychology, and sociology courses. Her particular field of interst is the history of women. Mrs. Mulford wrote the first Women's Studies curriculum for Livingston High School. She is the District Affirmative Action Officer.

Project Editors: Lynn Kloss, Karen Bernhaut, Ann Clarkson, Carol Schneider
Production Director: Kurt Scherwatzky
Production Editor: Alan Dalgleish
Editorial and Marketing Manager: Nancy Surridge
Editorial Development: WestEd, Ink
Electronic Page Production: Foca Company
Photo Research: Jenifer Hixson
Interior Design: Joan Jacobus
Cover Design: Joan Jacobus

Printed in the United States of America   3 4 5 6 7 8 9 10 01 00 99 98

ISBN: 0-835-91829-7

Globe Fearon Educational Publisher
A Division of Simon & Schuster
Upper Saddle River, New Jersey

CONTENTS

Ho Chi Minh led the Vietnamese in a struggle to drive out the French. By 1954, North Vietnam was an independent nation.

THE VIETNAM CONFLICT

TERMS TO KNOW
- legacy
- enlistee
- draftee
- defer
- Cold War
- parallel
- guerrilla warfare
- Green Berets

It was the spring of 1965. Seniors in a U.S. history class in York, Pennsylvania, were thinking about their upcoming prom and looking forward to their graduation. Lyndon B. Johnson was President. He had just won the election a few months before. But politics was pretty far from the students' minds.

When the teacher walked in, he seemed to be in low spirits. The teacher, a young man in his first year of teaching, looked worried. He started class by saying that the U.S. government had sent Marines to a small country in Southeast Asia called South Vietnam. Few of the students had ever heard of Vietnam. None of them could place it on a map.

The teacher said that that day's events would change their lives. Most of the students doubted it. Vietnam was thousands of miles away. How could it possibly affect them?

How wrong they were. Within four years, 18 students in the graduating class would be sent to Vietnam. Two would never return. Those who did return would find that they had changed tremendously. Few of them would ever again be as carefree as they had been that spring day in 1965, just before the senior prom.

1 The Heritage of the Vietnam Conflict

The U.S. Congress never declared war in Vietnam. The fighting was officially referred to as a *conflict*. However, once U.S. involvement increased, the conflict became more commonly known as the Vietnam War.

The Vietnam War changed people's lives all over the United States. Many people saw the war as a turning point in their lives. They divided their lives into two segments. The first part was what they believed before the conflict began. The second part was what they believed during and after the war.

The Vietnam War ended in 1975. Yet Americans still react to it with great emotion. To many Americans, the word *Vietnam* recalls a time when they were young. It recalls a time when Americans struggled with the burden of being a powerful country. It recalls often violent arguments over whether the United States had the right to interfere in another country's decision about the kind of government it should have.

The Vietnam conflict left a **legacy** that still exists today. A legacy is something that one generation leaves to another. The United States that completely withdrew from Vietnam in 1975 was a very different country from the one that in 1965 sent combat troops to Vietnam.

The original reason for sending U.S. troops to Vietnam was to stop the spread of communism. However, the Vietnam conflict caused Americans to reexamine their nation's conduct. Americans began to wonder if they could trust the people they had elected to high office. These changes in attitude still influence elections in the United States today.

U.S. forces tended to be young and "blue collar." Many soldiers were from minority groups. Here, in a 1968 ceremony, a U.S. Army captain administers the oath of service to a group of draftees.

A Responsibility to Serve

In the early 1960s, only military advisers were stationed in Vietnam. However, after 1964 the United States took a more active role in the civil war in Vietnam. Many young people believed that it was their responsibility to serve in the conflict. Others acted just as their parents had during World War II. Many believed, as one young man stated, that "our country is at war so it's my patriotic duty to go and fight."

In the beginning, many soldiers were **enlistees**. An enlistee is someone who volunteers to serve in the military. As the war continued, most new soldiers were **draftees**. A draftee is someone who is ordered by the federal government to enter the armed forces. Under the law, all males had to register for the draft, or Selective Service, when they turned 18.

During the Vietnam War, each local draft board had a quota, or maximum number, of young men it had to draft each month. Then, in the later years of the conflict, the government held a lottery. When a man's number was called, he had to go into the service. The average age of American soldiers drafted in Vietnam was 19. In World War II, the average age of the soldiers, or GIs, was 26.

A large number of draftees came from minority and working-class groups. African Americans, Latinos, and Native Americans were heavily represented. Young men from working-class families were also more likely to be drafted and sent to Vietnam. Vietnam was often referred to as a "blue-collar" war.

Unlike men from working-class families, young men from middle-class families were often able to escape the draft by going to college. Enrolling in college allowed these young men to put off their service until after graduation. Some young men were **deferred**, or excused, from the draft because they were married. However, President Johnson soon ordered the drafting of married men. Other young men were deferred because they were teachers or graduate students.

President Johnson also later ordered them drafted, except for certain groups, such as medical students.

A typical tour of duty in Vietnam lasted 18 months. Many men returned home after one tour of duty. Others signed up for a second and a third tour. Many re-enlisted when news reached Vietnam about the hostility that many Americans at home felt toward returning veterans.

During America's involvement in Vietnam, about 58,000 U.S. soldiers were killed. More than 300,000 Americans were wounded or injured during the war. About 5,000 were either prisoners of war or declared missing in action.

The War at Home

For Americans, there were two Vietnam conflicts. There was the war in Vietnam. But there was also "the war at home," as it came to be called. Anti-war protesters fought this battle on America's streets and college campuses, in the media, and even in homes, workplaces, and other institutions.

Except for the Civil War, no other issue divided Americans as much as Vietnam. Supporters of the war were called "hawks." Opponents were called "doves." A gulf of bitter feelings separated the hawks and the doves.

War protesters opposed the government by taking to the streets in small and large demonstrations. Some draft-age men burned their draft cards. Others refused to be drafted into the military and preferred to go to jail rather than join the military. Still others fled to Canada to avoid fighting a war that they believed was wrong.

Thinking It Over

1. What is the difference between an enlistee and a draftee?
2. What was "the war at home"?

2 The Beginning of the Conflict

The seeds that grew into the Vietnam conflict were planted at the end of World War II. World War II destroyed the old world order. It humbled great powers, such as Germany and Japan. Even some of the winners, such as Britain and France, found themselves weakened. The system of colonies was almost completely destroyed.

The Cold War

After World War II, the most powerful countries in the world were the United States and the Soviet Union. Many people hoped that these two superpowers could cooperate, as they had during World War II against Hitler's German army and mass killing of Jews. But the United States and the Soviet Union soon became bitter rivals.

The Soviet Union had a Communist government. It began invading Europe. In a number of countries in Eastern Europe, patriots had set up democratic governments after World War II. The Soviet army entered these countries and toppled their democratic governments. The Soviets replaced the democratic governments with Communist governments.

In 1949, democracy received another serious blow. In that year, China, the world's most populous nation, became a Communist nation. Populous nations are those that have many people.

After a long and bloody civil war, the Communists drove the non-Communists from mainland China. The Communists, led by Mao Zedung, took control.

U.S. leaders became concerned. They believed that the spread of communism was a threat to America. The threat of communism in America played a major role in the U.S. government's decision to send troops to Vietnam. The United States and other democratic nations began to build up their armed forces.

There was a long period of bad relations between Communist and non-Communist nations after World War II. During this period, the two sides made threats against each other. Each side built up its military forces and weapons, including nuclear weapons. There was fighting in some areas of the world. But there was not an all-out "hot" war. Therefore, this period of history is known as the **Cold War.**

Trouble in Southeast Asia

In the 1880s, France had set up colonies in Southeast Asia. Perhaps the most important of these colonies was Vietnam. During World War II, Japan took over the French colonies.

After Japan's surrender in 1945, France tried to regain control of these valuable colonies. Many of the Vietnamese people resisted. One of the leaders of the resistance was Ho Chi Minh, a Communist. In 1946, Ho Chi Minh declared Vietnam an independent country.

The French refused to accept Vietnam's declaration of independence. War broke out in 1946. Both sides expected aid from the United States. But because Ho Chi Minh was a Communist and had the backing of the Soviet Union, the United States backed France.

The war dragged on until 1954. In 1954, Vietnamese forces trapped French troops in a place called Dien Bien Phu. For two months, the Vietnamese tightened the noose around the French. Then in May, they attacked and defeated the French. More than 16,000 French soldiers became prisoners.

The Geneva Peace Conference

Also in 1954, a peace conference took place in Geneva, Switzerland. In July, the conference produced documents known as the Geneva Accords. The first accord, or agreement, stopped the fighting in Vietnam. It divided the country at the 17th **parallel**. A parallel is an imaginary east-west line on a map that shows a precise location.

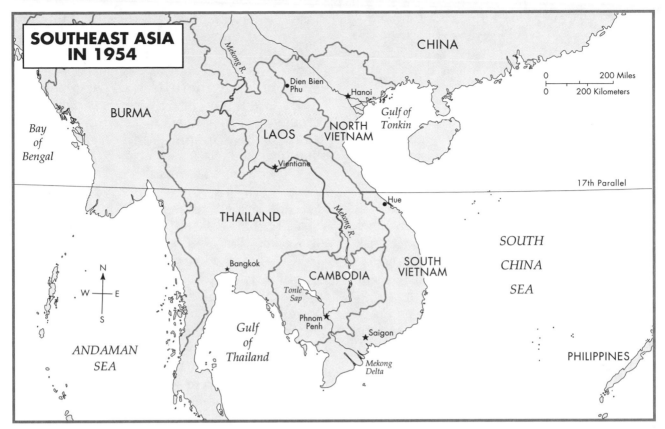

SOUTHEAST ASIA IN 1954

The settlement at Geneva in 1954 drove the French out of Indochina, creating the independent countries of Laos, Cambodia, North Vietnam, and South Vietnam.

After the Geneva Accords, the Vietnamese formed two separate governments. They called the Communist part of the country the Democratic Republic of Vietnam, or North Vietnam. Its leader was Ho Chi Minh. They named the part south of the 17th parallel the Republic of Vietnam, or South Vietnam. Its president was an anti-Communist named Ngo Dinh Diem.

The second Geneva Accord stated that the division of Vietnam was to be only temporary. It called for national elections to be held in July 1956. These elections were set up for the Vietnamese to determine a government for all of Vietnam.

The United States and South Vietnam refused to sign the Geneva Accords. Both governments were afraid that the Communists would win control of all Vietnam in free elections.

The Domino Theory

By 1956, the United States was concerned that communism was becoming too strong in Asia. China had become a Communist country in 1949. In 1950, Communist North Korea had invaded South Korea, an American ally. The United Nations voted to form a force to fight the invasion. The United States led this force. The efforts of this force prevented the fall of South Korea to communism.

The President of the United States in 1956 was Dwight David Eisenhower. He believed that Southeast Asia was the next target for the Communists. He was afraid that all of Southeast Asia was like a row of dominoes.

This concept soon became known as the "domino theory." Eisenhower feared that if the Communists took over Vietnam, its neighbors—Cambodia, Laos, and Thailand—would soon fall, too. Therefore, Eisenhower supported South Vietnam when it refused to go along with the Geneva Accords. Wanting communism to spread throughout Asia, China backed North Vietnam.

In 1956, President Diem refused to let South Vietnam take part in the elections called for in the Geneva Accords. He refused, he said, because honest, free elections were not possible in North Vietnam.

Diem was a dictator, yet he promised the Vietnamese people freedom and a better life. However, he never lived up to his promises. Bribery and corruption were common practices in South Vietnam's government. People who were willing to pay off government officials got the best government jobs and were awarded special favors. Many members of Diem's family received high-paying jobs in the South Vietnamese government.

Thinking It Over

1. What was the "Cold War"?
2. Name one of the terms of the agreement made at Geneva in 1954.

3 Fighting Begins Again

When the 1956 elections were canceled, Ho Chi Minh became convinced that only war could unify, or bring together, North and South Vietnam.

In South Vietnam, the people who opposed Diem formed what they called the National Liberation Front. Their opponents called them the Vietcong. After Diem refused to hold elections, the Vietcong formed an alliance with the North Vietnamese and began fighting the South Vietnamese government.

Because the South Vietnamese government had a large army and powerful weapons, the Vietcong used **guerrilla warfare**. Guerrilla warfare is a type of fighting in which small groups of rebel soldiers make surprise attacks against government soldiers and enemy buildings and bases.

Diem was a failure as a democratic leader. After John F. Kennedy succeeded Dwight Eisenhower as President in 1961, the United States continued to support Diem. Kennedy sent more economic aid to South Vietnam. He increased the number of U.S. military advisers from 2,000 to 15,000.

Many of the military advisers sent to Vietnam were members of the U.S. Army Special Forces. They became known as the **Green Berets**, because of the hats that they wore. Green Berets were not actually supposed to fight the Vietcong. They were sent to Vietnam to advise the South Vietnamese soldiers. Of course, when the South Vietnamese went into battle, their advisers did, too. The first American soldier killed in Vietnam was James T. Davis, a Tennessee Green Beret. He died in December 1961. This date was several years before the United States officially entered the conflict.

Despite the help of the Green Berets, the situation in South Vietnam worsened. By mid-1963, the Vietcong were so strong that President Kennedy faced a difficult decision. He would have to either send more soldiers and supplies to Vietnam or withdraw altogether.

Late in 1963, before Kennedy made this decision, two major events happened. On November 1, South Vietnamese generals killed Diem in a revolt against his government. The U.S. government knew about the revolt in advance. It had even pledged support to the generals.

Three weeks later, on November 22, 1963, President Kennedy was assassinated. Vice-President Lyndon Johnson then became President. The future of the Vietnam conflict was in Johnson's hands. He knew that Vietnam

Ho Chi Minh's first great victory came in 1954, when the French were ejected from North Vietnam. Here, neutral forces watch as the first Communist Viet Minh forces enter the capital city of Hanoi.

would be a key issue in the Presidential elections in November 1964—less than a year away.

An event in the summer of 1964 helped Johnson decide to send combat soldiers instead of military advisers to Vietnam—an attack at the Gulf of Tonkin. This attack is the subject of the first of eight case studies that follow.

This book tells the story of the Vietnam conflict. It describes some of the people who sacrificed their lives for what they believed. It tells about turning points in the war, such as the Tet Offensive. This book also tells about the terrible events that happened during the Vietnam conflict. One case study examines the massacre in the village of My Lai.

Other case studies describe the other conflict—"the war at home." Many Americans believed that the United States should not be involved in a civil war in another country. They demonstrated and protested to get the U.S.

government to change its policies. At Kent State University in Ohio, for example, National Guard troops killed four students during a protest of President Nixon's expansion of the conflict to Cambodia and Laos.

This book also describes the conflict through the eyes of the GIs who fought in Vietnam. Finally, this book will examine the legacy of the conflict and how it affected the United States.

Thinking It Over

1. Who were the Green Berets?
2. What event caused President Johnson to send combat soldiers to Vietnam?

Flanked by leaders of Congress, President Lyndon Johnson signs the Gulf of Tonkin Resolution. This resolution allowed Johnson to send U.S. troops to war in Vietnam.

ATTACK AT THE GULF OF TONKIN

CRITICAL QUESTIONS

- Is it a good idea to give a President unlimited freedom to act if he says that the United States has been attacked?
- Should the President be able to take military action without a declaration of war?

TERMS TO KNOW

- sonar
- retaliate
- resolution
- unanimously
- escalate

ACTIVE LEARNING

After you read this case study, you will write an editorial on the events that led to the passage of the Gulf of Tonkin Resolution in August 1964. As you read this case study, take notes to help you write your editorial. An editorial requires that you take a position on a key issue and defend it with facts.

In July 1964, a force of U.S. ships patrolled the waters off the coast of North Vietnam in the Gulf of Tonkin. The two biggest ships were aircraft carriers named the *Ticonderoga* and the *Constellation.* The *Maddox,* a destroyer, also patrolled with them that night.

Most of the sailors were young men with little combat experience. The majority had been sent to Vietnam after only six weeks of basic training.

"This Is Not a Drill!"

On the night of August 2, 1964, three North Vietnamese PT (patrol) boats raced through the water. Under cover of darkness, the North Vietnamese attacked the *Maddox.* They did not know that the *Maddox* had detected their boats on its radar screens.

During the battle, the North Vietnamese fired torpedoes at the destroyer. None hit. The *Maddox* fired its guns and hit one of the boats. Planes from the *Ticonderoga* damaged the other two enemy boats.

This attack was the first direct combat between U.S. and North Vietnamese forces. It lasted exactly 37 minutes.

1 We're Under Attack —Or Are We?

That night, Captain John J. Herrick, skipper of the *Maddox,* reported the incident to Washington. The next day, the U.S. government ordered the *Maddox* to patrol the gulf again. This time, a second U.S. destroyer, the *C. Turner Joy,* joined the patrol. The Navy warned Captain Herrick to be on guard and to expect further attacks by North Vietnamese ships.

Two days later, on August 4, 1964, the two ships cruised the rough waters. It was a dark night. Fog and mist made it difficult to see.

About 8:00 P.M., a radio operator aboard the *Maddox* intercepted radio messages from the North Vietnamese. Captain Herrick believed that the North Vietnamese might be planning another attack. Because of the darkness, Herrick called for air support. Soon eight jets from the *Ticonderoga* appeared to defend the *Maddox.* Neither the sailors nor the jet pilots could see any enemy ships.

Suddenly, there was a "blip" on the **sonar** screen. Sonar is a device that picks up sound

The U.S.S. Maddox, shown here on patrol in the South China Sea, reported an attack by North Vietnamese patrol boats. President Johnson used this report to win a free hand in dealing with North Vietnam.

waves bounced off objects in water. A young sonar operator heard some sounds that he couldn't explain. He reported that torpedoes were headed toward the ship. Captain Herrick immediately ordered the ship on a zigzag course to avoid the torpedoes.

"Contacts Appear Doubtful"

The eight fighter jets that were sent to defend the *Maddox* searched for 40 minutes. However, the pilots failed to locate any North Vietnamese PT boats. The *C. Turner Joy* reported that it had not picked up any torpedoes on its sonar.

Later, the U.S. government conducted an investigation. It questioned whether torpedoes had indeed been fired at the ships. Investigators noted that the crews were not combat veterans. In the excitement of their first battle, their minds could easily have played tricks on them.

Captain Herrick later investigated the sonar operator's report and believed that the sonar operator had made a mistake about the torpedoes. He thought that what the operator had heard was the sound of the ship's own propellers.

The day after the torpedoes were reported, Captain Herrick sent Washington officials a message about the second incident in the Gulf of Tonkin. The message said

review of action makes many recorded contacts and torpedoes fired appear doubtful. Freak weather effects and over-eager sonar operator may have accounted for many reports. No actual visual sightings by Maddox. Suggest complete evaluation before any further action.

All messages between the war zone and Washington were top secret. No one outside the

Helicopter gunships of the 173rd Airborne Brigade fire on Viet Cong positions outside the city of Bien Hoa. This attack was launched shortly after the attack in the Gulf of Tonkin. It marked a new phase in U.S. involvement in Vietnam.

White House learned about Herrick's memo until four years later.

Thinking It Over

1. Why was the U.S. naval task force on alert in early August 1964?
2. Why do you think the sonar operator believed that torpedoes were attacking the *Maddox* when no one saw any enemy ships?

Active Learning: Begin making notes for your editorial with a short summary of what happened in the Gulf of Tonkin. Remember that there were two incidents, two days apart. Write about the first incident. How did the ships respond to this attack? Then write about the second incident. What did the sonar operator hear? What did U.S. pilots find? What did the captain recommend to Washington?

2 A Call to Action

Reports of the second attack set off a flurry of activity in Washington, D.C. After the first incident on August 2, President Lyndon Johnson had been cautious. He had not **retaliated.** To *retaliate* means "to pay back an injury with another injury." Johnson decided that the North Vietnamese had attacked by mistake.

After reports of the second incident, Johnson sprang to action. Even though the information was questionable, Johnson announced to leaders of Congress that the North Vietnamese had attacked U.S. ships.

Just before midnight, Johnson appeared on national television. He told the American people that North Vietnam had attacked two U.S. ships. He said

> *renewed hostile actions against the United States in the Gulf of Tonkin have today required me to order the military forces of the United States to take action in reply.*

President Johnson ordered U.S. forces into action. That night, dozens of planes took off from U.S. aircraft carriers in the Gulf of Tonkin. They attacked targets in North Vietnam. U.S. planes destroyed fuel tanks and sank or damaged 30 North Vietnamese PT boats. This number was more than half of North Vietnam's fleet of PT boats.

The bombing raids against North Vietnam were costly. The North Vietnamese shot down two American planes and damaged two others. Lieutenant Richard Sather died when his plane was shot down.

The First American POW

On August 5, 1964, 26-year-old Lieutenant Everett Alvarez piloted an A-4 fighter-bomber over the Gulf of Tonkin. He was assigned to the aircraft carrier *U.S.S. Constellation.* Like other pilots aboard his ship, Alvarez was ordered to attack targets in North Vietnam. There had been many battle drills before, but that night was the real thing.

There were no stars to be seen. As Alvarez stood on the flight deck, he could see thunderstorms all around the area. Alvarez and the other pilots could only see the flight deck.

The deck crew attached thick steel cables to the plane. With the push of a button, the cables tightened and launched the plane. "It was like being held in the gut of an archer's bow," Alvarez said. Alvarez felt a surge of power as the plane bolted forward. It was like being shot from a cannon.

The A-4 quickly climbed to 30,000 feet. Alvarez was excited. He had been flying for four years. All of his training had been in preparation for that night.

In less than two hours, the jets neared the coast of North Vietnam. Until then, North Vietnam had been strictly off-limits. U.S. planes were not allowed to go near it.

The jets were flying at 500 miles per hour. The storm let up a little, and suddenly the pilots saw four North Vietnamese torpedo boats and a patrol ship. Alvarez fired his rockets. There was little time to see if any of the ships had been hit. As he looked back, he saw that the North Vietnamese were shooting at his plane. Flak, or gun fire, filled the sky.

The jets wheeled around in a huge circle. They were coming in for their second run. This run was always more dangerous than the first because they had lost the element of surprise.

In the middle of the second run, Alvarez suddenly heard an unusual sound followed by a yellow flash. His plane shook and started rattling and clanking. Smoke filled the cockpit. Alvarez shouted into his headphones: "I'm on fire and out of control!"

The plane started going down. Alvarez pulled the ejection ring. Seconds later, he was floating unharmed in the water. He tried to swim away toward the open seas, hoping that he would be rescued. But the current dragged him toward land.

A dark shadow loomed in the water ahead. It was a fishing boat. Alvarez held his breath, hoping that he would not be spotted. But a group of Vietnamese fishermen saw him and picked him up.

A few hours later, a North Vietnamese torpedo boat stopped the fishing boat. The North Vietnamese officers questioned Alvarez. They searched him and found his wallet. When they learned that he was an American, they became angry. The officers blindfolded Alvarez and locked him in a cabin on the boat.

Later, the officers put Alvarez in jail and questioned him. "Why did your planes come here to bomb and kill our people? Why?" a North Vietnamese officer asked Alvarez.

"To retaliate for your torpedo boat attacking our ships," Alvarez answered.

"You fool! There were no torpedo boats out there on the night of August 4. It is a lie! You have been used!" the officer angrily responded.

A Good Book to Read

Chained Eagle, by Everett Alvarez Jr. and Anthony S. Pitch. New York: Donald I. Fine, 1989.

Chained Eagle describes how the son of migrant California workers became an American hero. In this book, the first U.S. POW in North Vietnam recounts his years of imprisonment. After his release, Alvarez continued to serve his country. He joined the administration of President Ronald Reagan. Later, Alvarez became a successful businessman.

Johnson Goes to Congress

The night that Lieutenant Everett Alvarez was shot down, there were other disturbing reports. North Vietnam's army was reported to be gathering near the border of South Vietnam. Was North Vietnam getting ready to launch a massive invasion? Many military advisers thought that something had to be done—and fast.

On August 5, 1964, President Johnson sent a message to Congress. He asked Congress to pass a **resolution** of support. A resolution is a formal statement made by a group.

This resolution was quickly drawn up. It gave the President the power "to take all necessary measures to repel [fight off] any armed attack against the forces of the United States."

The first U.S. troops to serve in Vietnam were not soldiers, but advisers. Their mission was to help train South Vietnamese troops for battle, but they went into battle with the South Vietnamese.

There was no time limit on the resolution. Congress was going to give the President unlimited power.

Public Support

The American people believed that the North Vietnamese had attacked the two U.S. ships. They gave the President overwhelming support. Before the speech that explained why U.S. forces had been ordered into action, Johnson had been losing public support. According to one poll, his popularity rating was 42 percent. After the speech, it shot up to 72 percent.

Active Learning: Your editorial needs to state what the Gulf of Tonkin Resolution actually said. Study the terms of the resolution. Describe the most important points.

Congress Responds

The House of Representatives spent little time debating the Gulf of Tonkin Resolution. It **unanimously** approved this resolution, 416 to 0. *Unanimously* means "without opposition."

In the Senate, the vote was 88 to 2 in favor of the resolution. Senator Wayne Morse of Oregon was one of the two opposing votes. He suspected that the whole incident had been a "set up." In his view, the incident had been designed to push the United States into war.

Morse reminded the Senate that only Congress could declare war. Yet the resolution seemed to give that power to the President. Morse asked

Have we reached the point in American foreign policy where we are going to permit the President to send American boys to their death without a check by Congress by way of a declaration of war?

A few senators who voted for the Gulf of Tonkin Resolution also voiced their concerns. They also feared that they were giving the President too much power. Like Morse, they

Going to the Source

Then the Americans Came

Nguyen Thanh Mai was nine years old when the United States became actively involved in the Vietnam conflict. The account below describes the effect of the conflict on her family. She lived in North Vietnam.

The war started in the North in 1964, the fifth of August. At that time, I was nine years old, and lived in Dong Hoi. We knew when we were going to be bombed, and the children and older people were taken out the day before. My mother, a nurse, and my father, who was in the army, stayed in the city with my two older sisters.

I went to a village about twenty kilometers north, to a friend of my father. They bombed for only one hour that afternoon, but the whole city was destroyed. It was a very small city, very nice. In one hour it was completely destroyed.

We were lucky. My mother suffered from a concussion. She bled through the mouth. At the time, she was four months pregnant, and she lost the child. Everything was gone, our house, our possessions, everything. I remember, about ten weeks later I had a chance to return and I saw it once more—nothing.

We went to live near a forest, my family and all the other survivors, and we stayed there from 1964 until the liberation of the South. We were bombed nearly every day. You know, it was a very important place, about sixty, seventy kilometers north of the 17th parallel. The Northern soldiers passed through on their way to the front, and wounded people were being carried back.

We cut wood and built a house, but most of the time we stayed in a tunnel. The house was a façade [the front of a building], just somewhere to come out to sometimes. You may not believe how we were bombed nearly every day, sometimes three, four times a day. I had one friend—ten people in her family. Eight died. Only two sisters are still alive. I stayed in the village by the forest for seven, eight years and the bombing continued.

We got two kilograms of rice a month for five people. We had manioc [an edible root] and grew sweet potatoes. We had pineapples and other fruits, though sometimes our food was destroyed by the bombs.

From Martha Hess, *Then the Americans Came*
(New York: Four Walls Eight Windows, 1993), pp. 25–27.

1. What effect did the bombings have on Nguyen Thanh Mai's family?
2. Why didn't the family live in its house? Why did the family live in a tunnel instead?
3. Do you agree with the writer that "we were lucky" after the U.S. bombing attack? Why or why not?

stated that the U.S. Constitution gives Congress alone the right to declare war. Still, they voted for the resolution. They wanted to support the President in this time of crisis.

After the vote, Senator Morse told his fellow senators that they would live to regret their votes. "History will record that we have made a great mistake," he said.

Active Learning: For your editorial, decide whether you would support or oppose the Gulf of Tonkin Resolution. List the points raised in the text that support your position. Then support each point with details.

Thinking It Over

1. How strong was Congress's support for the Gulf of Tonkin Resolution?
2. Why do you think that the American public and Congress overwhelmingly supported President Johnson?

3 Tonkin Attack: A Fraud?

Was the second Gulf of Tonkin incident a set up? Was President Johnson looking for an excuse to attack North Vietnam? Later, many people came to share Senator Morse's concerns. They

Seated between Secretary of State Dean Rusk (to the President's right) and Secretary of Defense Robert McNamara (to his left), President Johnson debates a course of action after the Gulf of Tonkin attack.

wondered if the second attack on the U.S. ships had ever taken place.

One of President Johnson's private conversations suggests that it was indeed a set up. A few days later, in a conversation with one of his aides about the second gulf incident, Johnson said, "Those dumb sailors were just shooting at flying fish."

If Johnson believed his own statement, then why did he describe the incident as an attack on U.S. ships? Critics say that Johnson made the statement to get Congress to approve war without actually declaring war.

There is no doubt that the first incident on August 2 was real. North Vietnamese torpedo boats did attack the *Maddox* on the night of August 2.

Was Congress Misled?

Whether the second attack was real, President Johnson made the incident sound far more serious than it actually was. It is clear that he used the Gulf of Tonkin Resolution in ways that Congress had not intended.

To understand why President Johnson intentionally misled the American people, it is necessary to look back at what was happening in the United States in 1964.

The 1964 Election

One event on most people's minds that summer of 1964 was the election that would be held in November. Every four years, the United States holds a Presidential election. Americans vote for a President and a Vice-President, one-third of the Senate, and all members of the House of Representatives. There are also numerous state and local elections.

Everything that the President and Congress did that summer became an issue in the election. The civil war in Vietnam became the most critical issue of all.

A President Who Had Not Been Elected

In the summer of 1964, Lyndon Johnson was a President who had not been elected to office. He had become President less than a year before, on November 22, 1963, when President John F. Kennedy had been assassinated. Because he had not been elected, Johnson felt the need to continue Kennedy's policies.

One of the first actions that Johnson took as President was to call a meeting on Vietnam. All the top civilian and military officials came. They discussed how the conflict in Vietnam was going.

What they said in the meeting did not make the President happy. The conflict was not going well at all. Despite the presence of 16,000 U.S. advisers, the Vietcong were making steady gains against the South Vietnamese. In the first six months of 1964 alone, the Vietcong had seized 4,700 weapons from the South Vietnamese army. That amount was enough to equip ten Vietcong battalions. The North Vietnamese were secretly providing even more arms and supplies to the Vietcong in South Vietnam.

The South Vietnamese army was unable to defend its territory and government. It seemed ready to fall, unless it received help from other countries. This situation tested the United States's promise and willingness to fight communism.

Yet, during his first months in office, Johnson had sent only 5,000 new advisers to Vietnam. There was a good reason for this caution. The American people had made it clear where they stood. They wanted to defeat communism in Vietnam, but they did not want to send large numbers of U.S. troops to fight in Vietnam. Lyndon Johnson faced this problem during the summer of 1964. He needed to convince the American people that Vietnam was a cause worth fighting—and dying—for. But the American people were not convinced.

4 Johnson Gets a "Blank Check"

By the summer of 1964, the civil war in Vietnam was clearly growing worse. South Vietnam's government was unpopular. Its people seemed unwilling to continue the war. Johnson had three choices:

• The United States could pull its advisers out of Vietnam. This pull-out would probably result in the Communists' taking over Vietnam. But its neighbors—Cambodia, Laos, and Thailand—might fall under Communist control as well.

• The United States could limit its involvement. This choice pleased neither the "hawks" nor the "doves." The hawks favored more military support. The doves wanted to see an end to all fighting.

• The United States could **escalate**, or increase, its role in the conflict. The presence of U.S. combat troops would give South Vietnam time to strengthen its government.

The third choice—to escalate—was the path that Johnson believed he might have to take. But he would do so only after the 1964 election. In Johnson's view, U.S. troops would have to stay in Vietnam for only a short time. A stronger South Vietnamese army would then be able to fight on its own.

The incident in the Gulf of Tonkin gave President Johnson the power to escalate U.S. involvement in Vietnam. By making the incident at the Gulf of Tonkin seem much more serious than it had been, Johnson convinced Congress to give him important powers. He would not have to go to Congress to ask for a declaration of war. He could simply say that he was using the powers that Congress had already given him in its Gulf of Tonkin Resolution.

Armed with the Gulf of Tonkin Resolution, President Johnson met the North Vietnamese threat with a massive buildup of U.S. troops. Here, air mobile forces land at Vung Tau, South Vietnam, in early 1965.

Using the Resolution

In the meantime, the 1964 election continued. President Johnson attacked Barry Goldwater, the Republican Presidential candidate. Johnson said that Goldwater would expand the American role in the war. In October, just before the election, Johnson made a campaign promise he had no intention of keeping. He said that he would not send United States troops into battle in Vietnam. During his campaign, Johnson stated

> I am not about to send American boys away from home to do what Asian boys ought to be doing for themselves.

That November, Johnson was reelected by a huge margin. Just a few months later, in March 1965, Johnson ordered the first U.S. combat soldiers to Vietnam. He sent two battalions of Marines. He said that he was sending the Marines to protect U.S. bases. In fact, many of the advisers had already been involved in combat.

In July 1965, President Johnson admitted publicly that the American role in Vietnam had changed. He announced that U.S. troops would be actively fighting against the North Vietnamese. By the end of 1965, about 180,000 U.S. troops were in Vietnam. A year later, there were 400,000. At the end of 1967, there were more than a half-million U.S. soldiers in Vietnam.

The United States never declared war in Vietnam. The President never even asked for such a declaration. Instead, he used the powers given to him in the Gulf of Tonkin Resolution to escalate U.S. involvement in Vietnam.

Alvarez Returns

The action in the Gulf of Tonkin seriously affected many Americans. No one was more affected than Lieutenant Everett Alvarez. Shot down in the first air attack on North Vietnam, he was taken prisoner.

Alvarez remained a prisoner of war for the next eight-and-a-half years. The North Vietnamese kept Alvarez in a series of small cells. One cell was seven feet by seven feet. His captors beat, tortured, and sometimes starved Alvarez. At one point, Alvarez weighed less than 100 pounds.

On February 12, 1973, the North Vietnamese government freed Alvarez. By then, the Gulf of Tonkin incident had almost been forgotten. At the end of a conflict that the United States did not win, it had signed a prisoner release agreement with North Vietnam.

As Alvarez got off the plane in the United States, he saw an admiral. He saluted and said, "Lieutenant Everett Alvarez Jr. reporting back, sir."

Thinking It Over

1. What were President Johnson's three choices for dealing with the conflict?
2. If you had been one of President Johnson's advisers in 1964, which choice might you have supported? What advantages would this choice have over the others?

Case Study Review

Identifying Main Ideas

1. What happened in the first Gulf of Tonkin incident?
2. Why do some people now wonder if the second Gulf of Tonkin incident ever happened?
3. Why do you think that Congress passed the Gulf of Tonkin Resolution with so little opposition?

Working Together

Form a small group. Imagine that you are reporters at a press conference with President Johnson in 1964. Make a list of questions that you would like to ask President Johnson about the Gulf of Tonkin incidents. How do you think the President will answer your questions? Rehearse your answers and present them to the class.

Active Learning

Writing an Editorial Review the notes that you took as you read this case study. Write an opening paragraph that clearly states your position on the Gulf of Tonkin Resolution. In the next two or three paragraphs, state the reasons for your position. After writing your first draft, check it to make sure that it is clearly argued and free of mistakes. Revise it and prepare a final copy to turn in.

Lessons for Today

Many observers believe that there was more trust in government in 1964 than there is today. Charges of lying, or not giving all the details of an incident, were very unusual. Today we often hear charges that the government has lied to the American people. Why do you think that people are less trusting of the government today than they were in 1964?

What Might You Have Done?

Imagine that you are watching television late at night on August 5, 1964. An announcement interrupts the show that you are watching. It says that the President has an important message for the American people. He says that North Vietnamese forces have attacked U.S. ships in the Gulf of Tonkin. What thoughts are going through your mind? How do you respond?

Political Propaganda

Authors use many methods to persuade readers to agree with them. Sometimes authors use propaganda. Propaganda is the spreading of ideas to shape people's opinions. It is used to advance the cause of a group or to damage that of another group. Often it does both. Propaganda might contain half-truths and vague or misleading information. The following are some forms of propaganda.

Name-calling Name-calling is used to damage the image or reputation of a person or idea. For example, a political candidate might call another candidate dishonest.

Association Someone trying to hurt an opponent's image might associate, or link, the opponent with an unpopular idea or cause. The association might not be truthful. It also might not be plainly stated. Instead, it might be implied, or hinted at. For example, suppose a relative of a government leader has committed a crime. A political opponent may repeatedly draw attention to this crime to discredit the leader because of his or her association with the relative.

Jumping on the Bandwagon This technique is used to try to convince someone to do or believe something because "everyone else is doing it." Jumping on the bandwagon is similar to peer pressure.

Catch Phrases These phrases refer to things that most people favor. For example, a political candidate may claim to support the "American Way"—a concept that most Americans favor. However, the candidate may not be specific about what he or she means.

Critical readers pay careful attention to the words and phrases that people use. Critical readers evaluate an author's statements and arguments to determine whether the author is using propaganda.

Read the excerpt below. Then think about how the author uses propaganda to try to persuade the reader to agree with a certain point of view.

Some say that we should withdraw from South Vietnam, that we have lost almost 200 lives there in the last 4 years, and we should come home. But the United States cannot and must not and will not turn aside and allow the freedom of a brave people to be handed over to Communist tyranny. This alternative is strategically unwise, we think, and it is morally unthinkable.

Some others are eager to enlarge the conflict. They call upon us to supply American boys to do the job that Asian boys should do. They ask us to take reckless action which might risk the lives of millions and engulf much of Asia and certainly threaten the peace of the entire world. Moreover, such action would offer no solution at all to the real problem of Viet-Nam. America can and America will meet any wider challenge from others, but our aim in Viet-Nam, as in the rest of the world, is to help restore the peace and to reestablish a decent order.

From President Lyndon Johnson's
speech to the American Bar Association in
New York City on August 12, 1964
(Public Papers of the Presidents of the United States)

Answer the questions below. Review the excerpt to help you develop your answers.

1. What is the author's point of view regarding the conflict in Vietnam?

2. Are there ideas that the author hints at but does not express openly? If so, what are they?

3. How can you tell that the author is using propaganda?

4. What might someone with an opposing viewpoint say about the excerpt?

Recognizing Propaganda

Critical thinkers look for clues to help them recognize when propaganda is being used. To make a fair assessment of an idea or product claim, critical thinkers ask such questions as the following:

- Who is giving the information?

- What is the purpose of the information?

- What are the facts? How are the facts proven?

- What audience is targeted by the information?

- What images and phrases are used? What is implied by the images and phrases?

U.S. Marines take cover behind a fence in the city of Hue. A surprise attack during the Tet Holiday won the Viet Cong temporary control of the city.

THE TET OFFENSIVE

CRITICAL QUESTIONS

■ No one is sure who "won" the Tet Offensive. So why is it considered the turning point of the Vietnam War?

■ How did the Tet Offensive lead to the downfall of President Lyndon Johnson?

TERMS TO KNOW

■ cease-fire
■ psychological victory
■ reinforcements
■ grunts

ACTIVE LEARNING

After you read the following case study, you will be asked to interview someone who remembers the Vietnam War and the issues that surrounded it. As you read, think about the questions that you would like to ask. Remember that a good interviewer is a good listener. Your interview subject's answers will lead you to ask more questions.

It was January 30, 1968. Sounds of celebration in Saigon, the capital of South Vietnam, filled the warm night air. It was the second night of Tet, the Vietnamese New Year. The Vietnamese people name each year after an animal. In 1968, the people of Saigon were welcoming the Year of the Monkey with parades, feasting, and fireworks.

Saigon was peaceful. The war seemed far away. Happy crowds filled the streets. Overhead, the sky was lit with the sparkle of firecrackers. The South Vietnamese government declared a **cease-fire**. A cease-fire is a short pause when the opposing sides in a conflict agree not to fight. The South Vietnamese army allowed many soldiers to go home for the holidays.

At 2:00 A.M., 19 men met in a garage a few blocks away from the American Embassy in Saigon. These men weren't celebrating the holiday. They were Vietcong guerrillas. Along with thousands of their comrades, they had slipped into Saigon weeks before.

The men were dressed in ordinary clothes. They mingled with other Vietnamese travelers coming to Saigon for Tet. The Vietcong had smuggled guns, rockets, and explosives into the city before the beginning of the Tet holiday. They had hidden the weapons in carts of farm goods that passed right under the eyes of South Vietnamese soldiers.

The Vietcong's mission was to attack the American Embassy. The embassy was Saigon's most prominent symbol of America's role in Vietnam.

were killed. The guerrillas then used a rocket launcher to blast open the doors to the main embassy building.

The Americans inside the building kept up a steady stream of automatic fire to fight off the guerrillas. The Americans managed to keep the Vietcong from seizing control of the embassy building. U.S. Marines soon arrived. For six hours, there was a hide-and-seek battle in the darkness. After sunrise, U.S. soldiers rushed the gate and ended the fight.

By 10:00 A.M., U.S. soldiers had killed all 19 Vietcong guerrillas. But the guerrillas had controlled the grounds surrounding the embassy for more than six hours.

First Questions

U.S. television aired reports of the guerrilla attack on the American Embassy in Saigon. Americans were shocked at what they saw. Just four days earlier, General William Westmoreland, commander of U.S. forces in Vietnam, had been boasting. He declared that the Vietcong were "on the ropes"—a term that refers to a boxer who may soon be knocked out.

Another U.S. Army officer stated on January 24: "We begin 1968 in a better position than we ever have been before."

However, the television reports clearly showed that even the U.S. Embassy wasn't safe. The American situation in Vietnam was not as hopeful as Americans had thought or were told.

1 Attack on the American Embassy

At 3:00 A.M., the guerrillas attacked. They used explosives to blast a hole in the embassy's outer wall, and then they climbed through it. There was a brief exchange of gunfire. Two embassy guards and several of the Vietcong guerrillas

Active Learning: The Tet Offensive convinced many Americans that the conflict was not going as well as the U.S. government had been saying. For your interview, ask your interview subject when he or she became aware that the conflict was not going well.

As two U.S. military police lie dead in the foreground, their buddies take cover, waiting for reinforcements. The Viet Cong attack on the U.S. Embassy in Saigon took U.S. forces by surprise.

On the Attack

The attack on the U.S. Embassy was only a small part of the battle raging throughout South Vietnam. The leaders of North Vietnam decided to launch an offensive against all the major cities and towns of South Vietnam. The North Vietnamese and Vietcong would attack everywhere at once. They believed that a widespread attack would surprise U.S. troops. They also thought that the South Vietnamese army would crumble under the attack.

These attacks throughout South Vietnam became known as the Tet Offensive. The Tet Offensive became a turning point of the Vietnam War.

The South Vietnamese were completely surprised by the attack. Early risers in Saigon could not believe their eyes. While walking to work, they found Vietcong troops controlling some of the city's blocks. Groups of armed men moved quietly through the streets. Few believed that the Vietcong would dare to mass their forces for an attack on the cities.

Americans in Saigon were also taken by surprise. For three years, U.S. forces had pounded the Vietcong in battle. U.S. military leaders believed that the Vietcong had limited numbers of men and supplies.

Yet the impossible had occurred. More than 200,000 enemy soldiers were involved in the offensive throughout South Vietnam. The North Vietnamese and Vietcong attacked cities and towns from one end of South Vietnam to the other. Da Nang, a city with a large U.S. military base, was one of the first cities to be attacked. Then came Saigon, Hue, Dalat, and other cities.

General Giap

General Vo Nguyen Giap, a former teacher, was the mastermind of the offensive. He was the leader of North Vietnam's army.

Giap was famous for his earlier victories over the French. His greatest victory was at Dien Bien Phu. This 1954 battle convinced France that it could never control Vietnam.

Giap hoped for the same kind of victory over the Americans. He expected heavy casualties but thought that such a victory would force the Americans to leave Vietnam.

Giap had been planning the Tet attack for months. Thousands of his fighters had already been smuggled into South Vietnam's cities. The Communists had also smuggled in arms and supplies.

The North Vietnamese used many clever ways to sneak supplies into South Vietnam. In the week before Tet, for example, there was a sudden increase in funerals in Saigon. Most of the "dead" were brought into the city in coffins. Every day, the people of Saigon watched long lines of mourners marching through the streets to the cemeteries. Only after Tet did they find out that most of the funerals were fake. Instead of bodies, the coffins contained guns and ammunition.

Thinking It Over

1. Why did the attack on the U.S. Embassy in Saigon surprise Americans?
2. The Vietcong guerrillas who attacked the embassy were willing to die in the attack. In fact, none of them survived. Why do you think they were willing to sacrifice their lives?

2 The Battle of Hue

On the same morning that Saigon was attacked, North Vietnamese and Vietcong troops attacked almost 100 cities and towns in South Vietnam. Some of the worst fighting took place in the coastal city of Hue.

Many people considered Hue to be the most beautiful city in South Vietnam. Hue was not an important military center. It was an important cultural center. It was a place of learning and beauty. It had a large university and a high school where many South Vietnamese leaders had been educated.

Hue was also famous for its lush gardens and beautiful red, gold, and blue palaces. Lush tree-lined streets with wide green lawns were everywhere.

Hue had once been the home of Vietnam's emperors. The Imperial Citadel was located in the center of the city. This huge stone fortress was built in the 1800s. It had high, thick walls and covered two square miles.

One of the first targets of the Communists was the Imperial Citadel. The Communists knew that capturing it would be a powerful **psychological victory**. A psychological victory is a victory that is more important for the effect that it has on people's minds than for its military importance.

The Communists quickly pushed aside the city's U.S. and South Vietnamese defenders. They raised the red-starred Vietcong flag over areas that they captured. It didn't take long before the Communists controlled nearly every part of the city.

The fighting in Hue was very different from other fighting in the Vietnam War. It did not take place in the rain forest or in rice fields. Instead, it occurred on city streets and in alleys. Much of the shooting came from rooftops and doorways. Progress was measured street by street. Casualties were great on both sides.

Bloodbath

After taking over Hue, the Vietcong began one of the worst slaughters of the war. They compiled a list of people they intended to kill. The list contained the names of people who the Vietcong thought were working for the South Vietnamese

Street by street, house by house, U.S. troops tried to oust the more than 2,000 Viet Cong who had taken over the ancient city of Hue. When the battle was over, the once beautiful city lay in ruins.

government. It included government workers and members of the army.

Immediately after taking control of the city, Vietcong teams began a house-to-house search for the people on their list. One South Vietnamese woman described what happened to her father

My father was an elderly official about to retire. The Communists came to our house and questioned him. Then they took him away. My father never came back.

The Vietcong also killed soldiers home on leave, police, and office workers. They immediately shot some in the streets. Others received a brief trial before they were executed. To show their power, the Vietcong forced residents into the street to watch the "people's courts" pass death sentences.

During the months that followed the battle, a series of shallow graves was discovered. South Vietnamese officials and American soldiers found the remains of 2,800 people in the graves. Many of the victims had been shot in the head. Still others had apparently been buried alive. Many had had their hands tied behind their backs.

It is unclear who was responsible for the mass killings. But many survivors say that the Communist forces carried out the murders.

U.S. Forces Fight Back

Meanwhile, U.S. Marines began a military offensive. They intended to recapture Hue. In the fighting to retake the Imperial Citadel, one unit had one Marine killed or wounded for every yard of territory gained.

The weather was unusually cold and stormy. The troops had little or no sleep. There were few **reinforcements**, or troops sent in to help soldiers already under fire.

One American reporter described the mood of the Marines.

Going in, there were 60 of us in a truck. There had been a harsh, dark storm and it turned the route into a mud bed. Many of the houses had completely collapsed. Hundreds of refugees were on the side of the road as we passed. Many of them were wounded. The houses that we passed made good cover for snipers. All the **grunts** [infantry, or ground soldiers] *were whistling and no two were whistling the same tune. It sounded like a locker room before a game nobody wanted to play.*

More than 200 Americans died in the battle to regain control of Hue. About 1,200 were wounded.

The horrors of war were experienced throughout Hue. In this picture, people on their way to city shops hurry past the bodies of Viet Cong. The Tet fighting continued for weeks in cities such as Saigon, Hue, and Bien Hoa.

In the beginning, U.S. planes and heavy artillery, or guns, were kept out of action. Military leaders feared that the historic buildings in Hue would be damaged if heavy guns fired into the city, especially from the air. But it soon became clear that the enemy had dug in deeply. Then the South Vietnamese government gave the United States permission to start bombing. The bombings destroyed large sections of Hue.

There was fierce fighting. U.S. sharpshooters tried to strike enemy snipers who were firing from doorways and rooftops. Priceless treasures were destroyed in the battle.

Then, three weeks after they had entered Hue, the Communists retreated. South Vietnamese forces tore down Vietcong flags. In their places, they raised the yellow and red banners of the Republic of Vietnam, or South Vietnam.

Hue Is Destroyed

The battle for Hue was the longest battle of the Tet Offensive. It lasted four weeks. Both sides claimed victory. Communist forces were proud that they had held the city for more than three weeks. However, U.S. and South Vietnamese forces also claimed victory because, in the end, they held the city. They also boasted that the Communists had lost 5,000 soldiers.

The sure losers were the city of Hue and its people. The battle left more than half of the city damaged or destroyed. Out of a population of 140,000, about 116,000 people of Hue were left homeless.

Thinking It Over

1. Why did each side claim victory in the Battle of Hue?
2. Why did the Vietcong forces attack Hue, a city that was not an important military center?

Active Learning: Other battles were raging all over South Vietnam at the same time as the Battle of Hue. In your interview, ask your interview subject how he or she felt about the escalation of the war. Also ask how he or she felt about the rising opposition to the war in the United States.

3 Who Won the Tet Offensive?

By the beginning of March, the Tet Offensive had ended. The Communists had been driven out of the cities of South Vietnam. General Westmoreland proclaimed the Tet fighting a victory for the United States and South Vietnam.

In some ways, Westmoreland was right. The North Vietnamese and the Vietcong sustained terrible losses during the offensive. Even though the offensive was carefully planned, the Communists did not gain any new territory.

The Communists originally expected a general uprising among the South Vietnamese people against U.S. and South Vietnamese leaders. It did not occur. Most South Vietnamese viewed the Communists as brutal killers, not liberators. The South Vietnamese army did not crumble as the Communists had predicted.

Communist losses were tremendous. As many as 50,000 North Vietnamese and Vietcong soldiers may have died. Almost 52,000 were taken prisoner. About 2,600 U.S. and South Vietnamese soldiers were killed, and 12,000 were wounded.

But battles are not won or lost on the battlefield alone. The military victory won by the United States and South Vietnam was still a victory for the Communists off the battlefield. More than any other event in the war, the Tet

Offensive led Americans to question their country's role in Vietnam.

The Public Mood Changes

Before the Tet Offensive, the American public thought that the United States and South Vietnam were winning the war. Yet the Communists were able to attack nearly 100 cities and towns throughout South Vietnam.

After the Tet Offensive, there was a lot of pressure in the United States to end the war. More members of Congress called for a change in U.S. policy toward Vietnam. Senator Robert F. Kennedy, the brother of the assassinated President, changed his opinion on the war. He said that the Tet Offensive had shattered the optimistic views of Americans about Vietnam. Kennedy spoke for many Americans when he said

For the sake of those Americans fighting today, the time has come to take a new look at the war in Vietnam.

There are no formalities as a U.S. Marine kicks in the door of a house in Hue. Casualties were high during the house-to-house search for Viet Cong.

Major news magazines, such as *Time* and *Newsweek*, began to question the war. Opinion polls showed a sharp drop in American support for the war. For the first time, most Americans had doubts about the war and the reason that the United States was involved.

Americans Debate the War

The Tet Offensive revealed philosophical splits in the Democratic party over Vietnam. Both factions, or sides, criticized President Lyndon Johnson. The "hawks" wanted the President to use more force against the Communists. The "doves" wanted him to withdraw from Vietnam and begin peace talks.

Even President Johnson's closest advisers disagreed about what to do. General Westmoreland asked the President for about 200,000 more troops. This request set off an angry debate among Johnson's advisers because Westmoreland could not guarantee that the extra men would bring victory.

Johnson refused to send more men. He realized that the majority of Americans would no longer support the United States's ever-expanding role in Vietnam.

The Role of Television

Vietnam was the United States's first televised war. Americans watched the progress of the war every night on the news. CBS anchor Walter Cronkite was one of the most respected newscasters of that era. As news of the Tet Offensive was televised, he asked the same question that many Americans were asking: "What is going on? I thought we were winning the war."

Television brought the war into almost every U.S. home. But televised news has a weakness. It can oversimplify events. It uses pictures to tell a story. It does not always analyze the news. Television news showed plenty of fighting, bodies, ruins, and tears during the Tet Offensive.

But a viewer watching a street scene with homes burning might be misled into thinking

Going to the Source

A Letter from Vietnam

Lieutenant Frederick Downs Jr., from Kingman, Indiana, was a platoon leader in the 4th Infantry Division. He was wounded in action in January 1968 during the Tet Offensive. He wrote this letter to his wife Linda before he was wounded.

Here I am sitting down to write of my love for you and the horrors of war. Right now I'm pretending that I'm talking to you.

I can picture your face in front of me, and our home and our children. Oh! How much the things we take for granted can mean so much. The smell of cut grass, the wind blowing over the lake making the trees and grass sway. The smell of autumn, the bareness of the world during winter. All of this means so much, and how little it is appreciated.

In the mornings I put on my fighting gear: web belt with ammo pouches, hand grenades, smoke grenades, first-aid pouch, and canteen. Then I put two bandoleers of ammo around my neck so that it crosses my chest. Then comes my pack containing poncho, poncho liner, five C-ration meals, rain jacket, sweater, extra canteen, extra ammo, gun-cleaning kit, extra smoke grenade, an extra bolt for my rifle, a camera, and some cigarettes. Then I pick up my weapon and put on my helmet. With that on, I call my squad leaders and explain what my plan for the day is, based on what the captain passed down to me.

Mud, I never knew how much I could hate mud. We live in mud and rain. I'm so sick of rain that it is sometimes unbearable. At night the mosquitoes plague me while I'm lying on the ground with my poncho wrapped around me. The rain drips on me until I go to sleep from exhaustion.

This continues day after day until one wonders how much the human body can stand. And yet it is my job, and I do it willingly, knowing that war is a constant factor in this world. It has been so since the beginning of time. There is something that keeps us fighting past the time when we feel like quitting.

We go in tomorrow for sure. Everyone's morale is high, including mine. I'm looking forward to getting clean and relaxing. There should be some mail for me. I surely hope so. Letters mean a lot.

You know something, honey? I love you lots and lots. Only you know how much.

From *Dear America: Letters Home from Vietnam,*
ed. by Bernard Edelman (New York: Norton, 1985), pp. 60–61.

1. What hardships did Lieutenant Downs face every day?
2. Why do you think that he was willing to put up with all the hardships?

A Good Movie to See

Platoon, directed by Oliver Stone. Hemdale Film Corp., 1986.

This film won an Academy Award for Best Picture in 1986. It is about the life of a young soldier fighting in the Vietnam War. It shows how the war affected a young, middle-class college student who volunteered for the war. This film gives viewers an idea of what a soldier's life was like in Vietnam. It was made up of long marches, sleeplessness, bugs, and constant fear. This film is very realistic and powerful.

that a whole city or even the whole country was ablaze. It was not the whole truth. The news made Americans ask themselves such questions as "Can the United States and South Vietnam win the war?" and "Why is our country sending hundreds of thousands of its young men to fight and die in Vietnam?"

President Johnson recognized the power of television. He said in February 1968, "If I've lost Walter Cronkite, I've lost Mr. Average Citizen."

Public opinion shifted largely because of what Americans saw on television every night. Increasing numbers of Americans began to call for an end to the war.

Thinking It Over

1. Who do you think was the biggest winner in the Tet Offensive: the Communists or the United States and South Vietnam?
2. How could a battle be a military victory but a psychological loss?

4 Johnson's Big Surprise

President Johnson faced serious political problems—1968 was a Presidential election year. News of the Tet Offensive occurred just as candidates were beginning their campaigns.

As usual, the campaigns opened in New Hampshire with the first Presidential primary. Senator Eugene McCarthy, a critic of the war, challenged the President in the Democratic primary there. McCarthy was not well-known. Johnson had won the election in 1964 with the largest margin in history. Yet when the votes were counted in the New Hampshire primary, McCarthy had nearly won. He had received 42 percent of the votes compared to Johnson's 48 percent.

The election results stunned the President and the country. They showed that many people were against the war. Four days after the New Hampshire primary, Senator Robert F. Kennedy announced that he would challenge Johnson. He would also run for the Democratic nomination for President.

One of the issues raised by Johnson's critics was trust in the government. Many Americans believed that they had been fooled and lied to by the government. Many no longer trusted President Johnson or the government. Newspapers started calling the Vietnam conflict "Johnson's War."

"Step Toward Peace"

On March 31, 1968, President Johnson went on national television. Looking tired and upset, Johnson said, "Tonight I want to speak to you on peace in Vietnam and Southeast Asia." He announced that he was halting the bombing of North Vietnam. He asked Ho Chi Minh, North Vietnam's president, "to respond positively and favorably to this new step toward peace."

At the very end of his speech, the President had a big surprise. He said

I shall not seek and I will not accept the nomination of my party for another term as your president.

President Johnson's announcement surprised even his closest advisers. Johnson had not given anyone any sign that he was not going to run again. Many of his "Great Society" plans to improve the lives of ordinary Americans remained unfinished. But the war had taken a toll on Johnson. Public opinion polls showed that only 36 percent of Americans approved on his presidency.

After the Tet Offensive, only 26 percent approved of Johnson's handling of the war. Many large anti-war protests took place in cities and on college campuses across the United States. These protests convinced Johnson that he couldn't win reelection. He decided to seek peace in Vietnam rather than than try to win another four-year term.

Three days after Johnson's surprise announcement, the government of North Vietnam agreed to begin talking about ending the war. Almost all U.S. bombings in North Vietnam were halted. In May, delegates from the United States and North Vietnam met in Paris to start the peace talks. But there would be more than four more years of war for U.S. troops before the last U.S. soldier would return home. In January 1973 the United States signed a peace treaty with North Vietnam.

Thinking It Over

1. What two decisions did President Johnson make after the Tet Offensive?
2. Do you think that President Johnson's decision not to run for reelection was an act of courage? Explain your answer.

Active Learning: The spring of 1968 was a time of turmoil in the United States. President Johnson announced a halt to U.S. bombings in North Vietnam. He also announced that he would not run for reelection. In April, Martin Luther King Jr. was assassinated. In June, Robert F. Kennedy was murdered. Ask your interview subject what his or her response was to this news. Ask this person to describe the mood of the country at this time.

President Johnson, right, and his top advisers listen to a presentation by General Earle Wheeler on U.S. efforts to break the Tet Offensive. General Wheeler believed that the offensive had been a failure for the Viet Cong.

Case Study Review

Identifying Main Ideas

1. Why did the Communists consider the U.S. embassy a chief target of the Tet Offensive?

2. (a) In what ways was the Tet Offensive a victory for the United States and South Vietnam? (b) In what ways was it a victory for the Communists?

3. Do you agree or disagree with this statement: President Johnson was the biggest casualty of the Tet Offensive? Explain your answer.

Working Together

Form a small group. Make a display of photographs, drawings, maps, and other graphics about the key events of 1968, both in Vietnam and in the United States.

 ### Active Learning

Interviewing Review the questions that you wrote as you read this case study. Remember that your interview should focus on your interview subject's impressions of the war, not on his or her entire life. You want to give readers an idea of what the war was like from the perspective of someone who lived through it.

Lessons for Today

As you have read, some of the fiercest fighting of the war took place during the Tet Offensive. The goal of U.S. and South Vietnamese forces was to push back the enemy as much as possible. After a battle that completely destroyed the village of Ben Tre, an American officer said about this village: "We had to destroy it in order to save it." What do you think he meant by this statement? What is your reaction to this statement? The U.S. military received a great deal of criticism for this statement. What effect do you think this statement has had on U.S. military action since Vietnam?

What Might You Have Done?

This case study explains how television may distort the events that it is broadcasting. Imagine that you are working for one of the major television networks. Would you try to present a balanced and accurate picture of the war to viewers at home? Or do you think that sometimes television news should take sides in the coverage of the news?

Evaluating Conflicting Perspectives

People view the same events differently. The following are parts of two articles that appeared in U.S. newspapers shortly after the end of the Tet Offensive. Read them. Then, on another sheet of paper, answer the questions that follow.

The war in Vietnam is not winnable. The longer it goes on the more the Americans will be subjected to losses and humiliations.

Hard as it may be, the important thing now is not to pick up the challenge and charge in head down. On the contrary, the true national interest is to adjust our role to the realities. Unless we change our policies, then what has been happening in Saigon and elsewhere will be only a mild taste of the humiliations to come.

—columnist Joseph Kraft

We are already engulfed in warnings that all is hopeless in Vietnam because of the attack on the U.S. Embassy and the other Vietcong efforts in Saigon and other cities.

In reality, however, this flurry of Vietcong activities will almost certainly prove to have just the opposite meaning in the end.

It is certainly idiotic to go on talking about a war "with no end in sight," as so many do in this country, when the other side so obviously fears that a rather early end is in sight.

—columnist Joseph Alsop

1. What is Joseph Kraft's point of view? Which side does he think "won" the Tet Offensive?

2. What is Joseph Alsop's point of view? Which side does he think "won" the Tet Offensive?

3. How does each columnist think that the war will end?

4. How do you think it is possible for two "experts" on Vietnam to come to such different conclusions about the war?

5. Suppose that the two columnists had exactly the same information. Do you think that they could still reach different conclusions? Explain your answer.

The Language of Thinking

Critical readers identify key ideas while reading. Then they look for information that supports these ideas. Critical thinkers also consider an author's perspective, or point of view, and the author's purpose. For example, they ask themselves: *Is the author simply presenting information, or is the author also trying to persuade me to think in a certain way?*

Sometimes, people form conflicting opinions because they have different jobs. General William Westmoreland led U.S. forces in Vietnam. His job was to deal only with the military situation. General Westmoreland saw the Tet Offensive as a military victory for U.S. and South Vietnamese forces. But he believed that the war itself would be won only if 200,000 more American troops were immediately sent to Vietnam.

President Lyndon Johnson saw the Tet Offensive in a very different way. He believed that the offensive was the turning point of the war. Johnson understood that the Communists had been punished heavily. Yet he believed that they had won a great psychological victory. Therefore, Johnson decided not to send Westmoreland the extra troops that the general said he needed.

Study the questions below, and then answer them on another sheet of paper.

1. How did Westmoreland's background as a military officer shape his perspective?

2. President Johnson was a political leader. How do you think his position affected his perspective?

3. What were the political issues that Johnson considered? How did Johnson react to these issues?

4. Should political issues be considered when making military decisions?

5. Why do you think Johnson refused to send more U.S. soldiers to Vietnam?

6. Some people believe that the United States did not win the Vietnam War because it didn't use all the military power that it had. Some people say that the United States should have used nuclear weapons. What is your perspective on the use of nuclear weapons in foreign wars?

U.S. troops needed strong leadership to prevent soldiers from taking out their frustrations on civilians. Without that leadership, tragedies such as the My Lai massacre became a reality.

THE MY LAI MASSACRE

CRITICAL QUESTIONS

■ Does war make a person act immorally?
■ Who was to blame for the My Lai Massacre?

TERMS TO KNOW

■ hamlet
■ search and destroy
■ traitor
■ immunity

ACTIVE LEARNING

Many of the soldiers who fought in Vietnam kept diaries. A diary is an account of a person's life. Entries usually describe how a person feels about events that have happened in the person's life. As you read this case study, think of how you might have acted and felt if you were a soldier at My Lai, South Vietnam.

Charlie Company 1st Battalion, 20th Infantry, came to Vietnam in December 1967. Its men considered themselves to be the toughest unit in the 11th Brigade. When the brigade was sent to Vietnam, Charlie Company received a high honor. It was chosen to lead the 11th Brigade.

The company's commanding officer was Captain Ernest Medina. Charlie Company respected its captain. One of the company's men said: "He did everything for his men. His men always came first." Medina joined the Army in his teens. He wanted to make it his career. He was eager to go to Vietnam to prove himself.

Like Medina, most of the men were volunteers. Only a few had gone to college. They ranged in ages from 18 to 22.

One of Medina's platoon leaders was Second Lieutenant William L. Calley Jr. Calley was 24, but he looked much younger. One of his men said, "Calley reminded me of a kid, a kid trying to play war." A favorite expression of Calley's was "I'm the boss."

1 First Months in Vietnam

In January 1968, Charlie Company was sent to Quang Ngai province. This area is one of the most beautiful in South Vietnam. But to American soldiers during the war, it was also one of the most dangerous areas. The Vietcong had been in the area for 25 years. Most of the people living there were friendly to the Vietcong. Many U.S. soldiers had been killed there by booby traps and land mines.

Fighting against an unseen enemy with powerful weapons, U.S. troops took heavy casualties. Here, a wounded U.S. paratrooper is rushed to an evacuation helicopter during a 1969 fire fight for a hill nicknamed "Hamburger Hill."

Going to the Source

Brian Sullivan's Letter Home

Brian Sullivan was a lieutenant in the U.S. Marines. He wrote the following letter home to his wife in 1969. The letter describes his growing weariness and despair. Today Sullivan lives in New York City.

March 2, 1969

Darling,

After all these endless days and nights, they gave me and the platoon 36 hours off. I spent today going to memorial services for my people, doing wash, catching up on my work in my office, and writing up people for medals.

These last few days were so filled with fighting, marching, thinking, all the time thinking "Am I doing it right?" "Is this what they said at Quantico [the Marine training base]?" "How can I be sure I haven't led us into a trap, and the NVA [North Vietnamese Army] are waiting?" I'm just so grateful—to whom?—I "only" lost six men. I know how awful that sounds.

I'm so confused. At the services today, they were talking about God protecting people and eternal life and I felt so desolated, so despairing. . . . I began crying. I felt so awful and hopeless, but somehow held it back, and it just looked as if it was sniffling from my cold. See how awful my ego and pride are that I couldn't even let myself weep for those poor, poor kids.

Again, though it may be foolish, I'll keep my word and be honest. The post-Tet offensive isn't over. All intelligence points to a return bout. However, my platoon is 100 percent better than it was. We have so much rapport [unity] now, like a family, really. We'll all watch out for each other.

Brian

From *U.S. News and World Report*, Nov. 12, 1984, pp. 68–69.

1. How did Lieutenant Sullivan spend his time off?
2. What effect did fighting have on the members of Lieutenant Sullivan's platoon?
3. How do you think soldiers like Lieutenant Sullivan felt about the war protesters?

In their first few weeks, the company saw little action, although sometimes it had to arrest civilians. Both Medina and Calley were convinced that most of the people in the province were Vietcong. The other men in the company had the same attitude. Soon they began to view all Vietnamese as their enemies.

Later, as the unit patrolled the region, Vietcong snipers fired on the unit. The snipers wounded and killed several of the men. Each time one of the men was shot, the soldiers' anger toward the Vietnamese grew. As the weeks went by, the soldiers became tired. Their morale was low. They began to take out their anger on the Vietnamese. They beat prisoners, who were often children and elderly people.

On February 25, Charlie Company suffered its worst day. The Vietcong killed six men and seriously injured 12. One of the men summed up the feelings of the group. He said, "Okay, you guys [the Vietcong] want to be tough. We can be tough right with them."

Active Learning: To begin writing your first diary entry, think about how you might feel if an enemy that you couldn't see was killing your friends.

The Attack on My Lai

Early on the morning of March 16, 1968, Charlie Company lined up on a landing field, waiting for its helicopters. Their target was less than 15 minutes flying time away. The destination was the **hamlet**, or small village, of My Lai.

The pilots made their final approach to the landing zone. Gunners on board fired the first shots of the day on the village. The people of My Lai fled underground into crude bomb shelters or tunnels. The soldiers of Charlie Company were also frightened.

As they hit the ground, Calley shouted, "Let's go!" Everyone jumped out. The helicopters kept firing on the village with machine guns and rockets. Surprisingly, the enemy did not return fire. Most of the villagers hid from the U.S. soldiers.

Thinking It Over

1. What was the attitude of Charlie Company toward the Vietnamese people?
2. Why were many of the U.S. soldiers afraid and frustrated?

2 Massacre

For the next three hours, Charlie Company moved through the area of My Lai, which was not just one little hamlet. It included many small pockets of homes grouped together. The soldiers' mission was to **search and destroy**. This type of mission is an intensive scouring of an area to kill all enemy troops there.

Confusion About Their Orders

There was a great deal of confusion about what Captain Medina's orders actually were. One soldier reported that Medina "ordered us to kill everything in the village." Another said that the captain told them

Well, boys, this is your chance to get revenge on these people. When we go into My Lai, it's open season. When we leave, nothing will be living. Everything's going to go.

But other soldiers remember the orders differently. They said that Medina never ordered them to slaughter the people. They heard him say to destroy the village and to make sure that no one could live there anymore.

Calley's Platoon

Lieutenant Calley's platoon was heavily armed. He led the way. Calley and his men quickly took control of the landing zone. There was still no enemy fire in the area. Calley and his men moved toward the village.

About 700 people lived there. Most of them lived in thatch-covered huts. The soldiers called them "hooches." A large plaza was in the center of My Lai. Calley and some of his men walked into the plaza area. No one in the plaza tried to run away. They knew that if they ran, the soldiers would think that they were Vietcong and would shoot them. There was no sniper fire and no sign of any large enemy unit.

A man named Do Chuc was eating breakfast with his family when the GIs entered the village. The GIs marched the family and the other villagers to the plaza. Once there, they were told to squat. Chuc said, "We had no reason to be afraid. Everyone was calm."

The Killings Begin

The killings began without warning. U.S. soldiers fired on any fleeing villager. Soldiers yelled inside the huts for people to come out. If no one answered, they threw grenades into the hut. Calley's troops gathered small groups of people. There were about 50 or 60 elderly men, women, and children in the plaza. A few of them yelled out, "No VC [Vietcong]. No VC."

Calley raised his weapon and started shooting. He ordered his men to do the same.

No modern war spares civilians, but the Vietnam War had a particularly high number of civilian casualties. Here, a South Vietnamese soldier tries to save a civilian after a truck has hit a land mine.

They fired hundreds of bullets until they had killed all of the Vietnamese they had found.

One of the GIs later explained what he thought happened that day

> We were all psyched up, and as a result, when we got there the shooting started, almost as a chain reaction. The majority of us had expected to meet VC combat troops, but this did not turn out to be so. I guess you could say that the men were out of control.

After the slaughter in the plaza, Calley's platoon moved through the village. They killed anyone who moved. One of the victims was a Buddhist monk. Calley kept asking him questions. "Where are the Vietcong? Where are the weapons?" The old man answered that there were no Vietcong soldiers or weapons in the village. Calley became angry. He grabbed the monk, threw him on the ground, and shot him.

The soldiers brought the Vietnamese who had not been killed right away to a large ditch on the east side of My Lai. Soon, there was a group of about 75 Vietnamese in the ditch. They were mostly women, elderly men, and children. They were afraid and kept trying to get out. Calley began shooting and ordered his men to join in. One soldier later admitted, "I shot maybe 25 or 20 people in the ditch."

In other parts of My Lai, GIs burned huts, slaughtered animals, and destroyed food. By early afternoon, My Lai was no more. Huts had been burned to the ground. Buildings had been turned to rubble. Almost all of the My Lai villagers were either dead or dying.

Thinking It Over

1. What is a "search and destroy" mission?
2. Describe Charlie Company's mission in My Lai.

Seeing close comrades killed or injured by the unseen enemy angered U.S. troops. Some soldiers blamed the villagers for the violence.

Active Learning: Ask yourself how you might have reacted to the My Lai massacre. Do you think you might have joined in the killing? Might you have tried to stop the killing?

3 After the Massacre

After Charlie Company left My Lai, rumors spread about what had happened. Many soldiers knew that it had been terrible. It was surprising that only three weapons were found. This fact was difficult to believe because, according to its officers, the unit had killed 128 Vietcong.

American generals heard, but didn't want to believe, the rumors of a massacre. One of the generals suggested that the matter should be kept quiet.

One helicopter pilot saw the shootings and reported what he had seen. Early on the morning of March 16, Warrant Officer Hugh Thompson flew low, circling the area near My Lai. Everywhere he looked, he saw dead civilians. He radioed headquarters. He described "wild shooting by men on the ground."

An investigation began quietly. The commander of the brigade said

> I talked to about 40 [of the soldiers of Charlie Company] and asked them point blank if there was any truth to these reports. I got a negative from all of them.

When news reporters questioned the commander, he said that he was satisfied with the answers that he had received from Captain Medina and the men of Charlie Company.

The official report stated that the charges and rumors of a massacre were "obviously a Vietcong propaganda move." It claimed that the Vietcong were trying to make the United States look bad in the eyes of the Vietnamese people. The investigation ended.

Charlie Company Gets an Award

Three weeks after the attack on My Lai, General Westmoreland gave Charlie Company an award. American officers called the mission a great success in the war against the Vietcong. Captain Medina was praised for his "quick response." Even *The Stars and Stripes,* the Army's newspaper, reported that the attack on My Lai had been a stunning success.

A few men in Charlie Company were upset by the My Lai massacre. But they kept quiet. As one soldier said, "Everyone was afraid to tell the truth." General Westmoreland visited the unit soon after the incident. The brigade's leaders chose not to tell him about the rumored killing of civilians at My Lai.

The Vietnamese Reaction

South Vietnamese officials soon learned about the killing of civilians at My Lai. The few survivors reported that U.S. soldiers had shot about 500 villagers. But the South Vietnamese officials were in a difficult spot. The Americans were their friends and allies. If the officials reported the slaughter, the Americans might think that the officials were disloyal. The officials chose not to believe the stories and, instead, stated that the reports were lies that the Communists were spreading.

A few weeks after the incident, the Vietcong picked up the story. Vietcong soldiers wore red arm bands that said, "Remember My Lai." They handed out leaflets charging the American soldiers with brutality.

Because the U.S. and South Vietnamese governments believed that the attack on My Lai was a lie, any South Vietnamese who agreed with the Vietcong account of what had happened was accused of being a **traitor** to South Vietnam.

Warrant Officer Hugh Thompson, a helicopter pilot, reported seeing civilian bodies around My Lai. He filed an official complaint, but an investigation concluded that there had been no massacre.

A traitor is someone who is disloyal to or betrays his or her country.

All the officers involved in the mission wrote reports. Many left out important details. One officer claimed that civilians had been killed because they had been caught in the cross-fire between U.S. and Vietcong forces.

But the story of the massacre refused to die. More and more details slipped out. One concerned American finally made the American public take notice of the story.

Ron Ridenhour's Search for the Truth

Ron Ridenhour was a member of a helicopter crew in Vietnam. He had heard stories about the massacre and decided to fly over My Lai a few days after the raid. He remembered thinking that there were no signs of life anywhere.

At the end of April, Ridenhour met up with an old buddy. They hadn't seen each other for

months. The friend spoke about My Lai. He said that his unit had gone into the village and killed everyone.

Ridenhour was horrified. He had seen civilians murdered before. However, he had never seen slaughter on the scale of My Lai. The more he learned, the angrier he became. He decided to try to discover the truth.

Ridenhour questioned others who had been at My Lai. Soon he had a pretty complete picture. In December 1968, Ridenhour went home. With tears in his eyes, he told his family about the massacre at My Lai. He didn't know what to do next.

On April 2, 1969, Ridenhour wrote a three-page letter describing the "dark and bloody" attack on My Lai. He sent the letter to President Richard Nixon, 30 government officials, and numerous members of Congress.

Ridenhour believed that it was no longer possible to cover up what happened at My Lai. In mid-April, the U.S. Army began a full-scale investigation of the My Lai incident.

Thinking It Over

1. What did the first investigation of My Lai find?
2. How did the official report explain the large number of civilian deaths?

4 The Uncovering

Colonel William Wilson was in charge of the early investigation. Wilson traveled throughout Vietnam and interviewed most of the members of Charlie Company. Many talked openly because they felt guilty about what had happened at My Lai. They wanted to tell the truth. They wanted to explain why they had done what they did.

Wilson then spoke to Captain Medina. The captain protested. He said that he had been cleared by the earlier investigation. Wilson tried to get the official files of the earlier investigation, but the files had disappeared.

There was, however, enough evidence to order Lieutenant Calley home from Vietnam. In June, Calley appeared in a line-up. He was identified as the officer who had shot the civilians by the ditch. More and more evidence was collected about the massacre. It became obvious that the Army was going to put Lieutenant Calley on trial. One official said

> If they don't prosecute somebody for this, the Army is going to get clobbered. And if the story ever breaks without the Army taking action, it would be even worse.

Wilson sent his final report to General Westmoreland. Westmoreland ordered the investigation continued. Investigators located Ronald Haeberle, who had worked as a photographer at My Lai. He had color pictures of the shootings. Using the pictures, investigators interviewed former Charlie Company members again. The photos jogged memories, and more details came out.

Calley Is Charged

On September 5, 1969, Lieutenant Calley was charged with murdering a total of 109 My Lai villagers. Initially, Calley refused to testify against Captain Medina, his commanding officer.

News reporter Seymour Hersh researched the story. *The New York Times* was very interested in Hersh's report. The *Times* then sent reporters to Vietnam to investigate the killings. A reporter interviewed survivors of My Lai. The survivors told the reporter that Americans had killed 567 Vietnamese. Soon all the major U.S. news magazines began their own investigations. Everyone was suddenly talking about My Lai.

Lieutenant William Calley commanded the platoon that entered My Lai on that fateful day in March 1968. Found guilty of murder in 1971, he served two years in prison and was later paroled.

The Trial Begins

Calley's trial lasted for over four months. The trial was held in a small courthouse at Fort Benning, Georgia. The jury was made up of six Army officers. All of them had been in combat. The judge was a 25-year Army veteran.

More than 100 witnesses were called, but some refused to testify. They said that the Constitution protected them. The Fifth Amendment to the Constitution states that people do not have to testify if what they say can be used against them in a court of law. Others were given **immunity** in exchange for their testimony. *Immunity* means "the government agrees not to punish a person for what he or she did, even if the person is guilty of a crime."

Witnesses described the mass killings in court, and several described Calley's actions.

Calley's Defense

George Latimer defended Calley. Latimer had once served on the Utah Supreme Court. He said that he liked Calley right from the start. "Why, he could have been my son," Latimer said. He decided to take the case as a matter of principle.

Calley's defense was that he was only following the orders of a higher-ranking officer. Latimer said that Calley wanted to please Captain Medina.

If he [Medina] *had ordered Bill* [Calley] *to lead the platoon up a mountain and jump off it, he would have done it.*

On the stand, Calley defended himself. He said, "I was ordered to go in there and destroy the enemy. I did not sit down and think in terms of men, women, and children."

After all the witnesses had been heard, the case went to the jury. For 13 days, members of the jury considered all the evidence that they had heard. On March 29, 1971, they found Calley guilty of killing 22 villagers.

Two days later, the judge sentenced Calley to life in prison. He stayed in jail for only three days. On the fourth day, President Nixon freed Calley from prison. He was put under house arrest while his case was appealed. After review of the case, Calley's sentence was reduced to twenty years at hard labor. Later in 1973, a special Army board recommended reducing

A Good Book to Read

Fallen Angels, by Walter Dean Myers. New York: Scholastic, 1988.

Award-winning writer Walter Dean Myers wrote a riveting and realistic portrayal of the Vietnam War. The book focuses on five grunts—Richie Perry, Lobel, Johnson, Brunner, and Peewee. All five soldiers went to Vietnam for different reasons, but they all had the same goal—to get out of Vietnam alive.

the sentence further. On November 9, 1973, the Secretary of the Army announced that Calley would be paroled. He was released and given a dishonorable discharge from the Army.

Thinking It Over

1. What do you think happened to the official file of the earlier investigation?
2. What was Lieutenant Calley's defense?

Case Study Review

Identifying Main Ideas

1. Why did some U.S. soldiers consider all Vietnamese people to be their enemies?
2. Why do you think that the soldiers were ordered on a "search and destroy" mission at My Lai?
3. What were the charges against Lieutenant Calley?

Working Together

Form a small group. Write a series of television news broadcasts that tell the story of My Lai—from the incident itself to the release of Lieutenant Calley—as it might have appeared on television in 1967. Write what people would have known then, not what people know today.

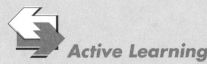

Active Learning

Writing a Diary Entry Review the notes that you took as you read this case study. Start your diary entry. Remember that a diary is written for yourself. Tell what happened at My Lai. What feelings and emotions did you have? How do you feel about the other soldiers in your unit?

Lessons for Today

We all think that we know right from wrong. Most people think that they can behave in a moral way no matter what is happening around them. But war does strange things to people. How does this statement apply to the My Lai massacre? Are you surprised that many Americans in the 1970s considered Calley a hero? Think of situations in your own life and in school life in which you have to make difficult choices. Do you always choose what is moral? Why or why not?

What Might You Have Done?

Imagine that you witnessed the events at My Lai. Do you think that you would have reported the massacre of civilians? This report might have gotten your unit and its members into trouble. Would you have kept quiet? Keeping quiet would have made you a party to the wrongdoing. What might you have done?

CRITICAL THINKING
Developing the Courage to Fight Unfair Treatment of Others

Intellectual courage is the ability to keep an open mind and not to allow others to make up your mind for you. By honestly considering other points of view, you remain fair. Being fair-minded helps you recognize the truth. Read the information below. Then respond to each question that follows.

A Few Who Had Courage

The soldiers of Charlie Company killed the people of My Lai because most of the soldiers did not question their orders. They didn't protest the killing of civilians. Most of the soldiers viewed all the people as Communists and enemies. Some of the soldiers were horrified. But most were too afraid to do or say anything.

However, a few soldiers did take risks to help the South Vietnamese. The soldiers' consciences told them that what Charlie Company was doing was wrong. Those who helped the people of My Lai to survive risked their lives. These few people had courage. One helicopter pilot witnessed the slaughter. He landed his helicopter and threatened to shoot his fellow Americans if they didn't stop the killing.

1. If most people around you are sure of something, why is it difficult to question or disagree with them?

2. Is it ever a good idea not to question or disagree with others? When and why?

3. Why is it difficult to question your own beliefs?

Have you ever changed a belief? Copy the chart below on a separate piece of paper and use it to describe what you once believed and what you now believe.

Used to Believe	Believe Now
1.	1.
2.	2.
3.	3.

Deep in the Cambodian rain forest, a U.S. Army staff sergeant checks a map to find his position. The May, 1969, raid into Cambodia set off a firestorm of opposition to the war.

THE SECRET WAR IN CAMBODIA

CRITICAL QUESTIONS

■ Why do U.S. Presidents often have trouble keeping their campaign promises?

■ Should all military actions be fully publicized?

TERMS TO KNOW

■ neutral

■ sanctuary

■ incursion

ACTIVE LEARNING

After reading this case study, you will write a newspaper article on the events that took place in Cambodia in 1969 and 1970. Take notes as you read to help you write the article. Remember that good newspaper articles answer each of the "Five Ws": Who? What? When? Where? and Why?

President Richard M. Nixon addressed the nation in a televised broadcast in April 1970. He spoke from the Oval Office in the White House. As Nixon was speaking, Americans had already begun firing guns in Cambodia, which borders Vietnam. There was not supposed to be any fighting in the country. Even so, an air strike over Cambodia had started.

President Nixon sat at his desk, pointing to a map of Southeast Asia. He said that the young GIs following his orders were all ready to move out. An invasion of Cambodia was on.

Nixon's speech explained the military's reasoning behind the invasion. He announced that military officers had known for a long time that North Vietnamese and Vietcong were using sites in Cambodia as secret military bases for the war against South Vietnam.

Earlier that spring of 1970, American B52s dropped countless bombs into Cambodia. The Communists lost many soldiers, food, and equipment. Yet, it didn't take long for the Communists to rebuild their forces. Nixon meant for the invasion to wipe out the Communist bases once and for all.

The American force was enormous. On May 1, 1970, the invasion of Cambodia began. Thousands of U.S. soldiers entered Cambodia. They were protected by hundreds of artillery shells, which rained down on the North Vietnamese and Vietcong bases. In one period of six and one-half hours, Americans fired 2,436 shells at the enemy.

The U.S. Eleventh Cavalry crossed the border into Cambodia at 10 A.M. It moved north along Route 7 all day. The soldiers struggled in the tropical heat. They moved slowly and carefully. A thick covering of trees was on both sides of the road. As the soldiers moved through Cambodia, they could barely see in front of them. The rain forest was a good hiding place because it was very dense. Several times the soldiers came to small rivers only to find that the enemy had blown up the bridges.

Some American helicopters flew above the soldiers. Their job was to find the North Vietnamese and Vietcong military bases. On the fourth day, they got lucky. The Americans spotted a large enemy camp that they called "the city."

The next morning, the first American troops entered the camp. They were stunned by what they saw. The soldiers found a huge complex of buildings concealed in the middle of the rain forest. The complex included 182 storage areas and 18 dining halls. Soldiers found tons of rice packed in storehouses. But they could not find any Communist soldiers. The

Under the dense cover supplied by the rain forests of Cambodia, the North Vietnamese used the Ho Chi Minh Trail to supply their troops throughout South Vietnam.

enemy had fled into the rain forest just hours before the U.S. troops arrived.

Still, the Americans were not disappointed. They hoped that the enemy's loss of food and supplies would prevent the enemy from starting a new offensive. If the invasion of Cambodia reduced the number of GIs killed or wounded, then American officers would think that the invasion had been worthwhile.

1 President Nixon's War

Sixteen months earlier, in January 1969, Richard M. Nixon, had taken office. Nixon knew that an all-out military victory was not likely in Vietnam. Instead, he said that he had a plan to win what he called "peace with honor." His plan was to pull the United States out of the war slowly. But it would do so in a way that would show the world that the Americans had not lost the war. South Vietnam would not be abandoned. Nixon believed that the rest of Southeast Asia would be in danger if the United States simply left Vietnam.

After Nixon took office, the war continued. But he slowly began to reduce the number of American troops in Vietnam. However, at the same time, Nixon decided to "teach the North Vietnamese a lesson." He wanted to show them that the United States would set the terms for peace.

Nixon and his advisers decided on a surprise move. The President approved a plan to bomb Communist supply bases in Cambodia.

Cambodia's mountains and rain forests had provided shelter for a secret road from North Vietnam into Cambodia. The enemy used the road to bring soldiers and supplies south from

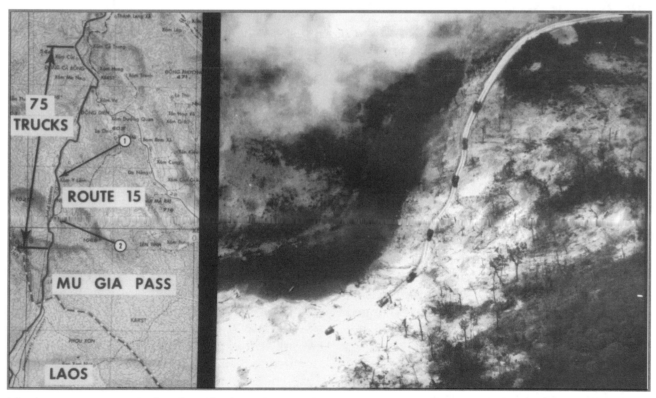

North Vietnamese trucks head south along the Ho Chi Minh Trail with soldiers and supplies for the Communist war effort.

North Vietnam. Americans called this road the Ho Chi Minh Trail.

Bombing the Ho Chi Minh Trail was not a new idea. U.S. and South Vietnamese forces had already been bombing other sections of the road. What was new was that the bombing would extend into South Vietnam's neighbor—Cambodia. Cambodia was a **neutral** country. Being neutral means not taking sides.

For years, Cambodia had tried to stay out of Vietnam's civil war. But the Communists had often violated Cambodia's neutrality. They used the rain forest to supply their forces. They set up camps where their soldiers could rest, treat their wounded, and prepare for future battles. These areas were called **sanctuaries**. A sanctuary is a safe place that cannot be attacked. The Communists thought that these bases were safe because they knew that the United States could not enter into or bomb Cambodia.

The Nixon Strategy

In February 1969, just a month after Nixon took office, the Communists began a new Tet offensive. Nixon thought that the Communists were testing him. He decided to put more pressure on them by approving the military request to bomb Cambodia.

The bombings lasted for 14 months. U.S. bombers raided Cambodia 3,695 times. The goal was to destroy the enemy's supply routes.

The air raids over Cambodia were given the code name "Menu." Target areas were called "Breakfast," "Lunch," "Dinner," "Supper," "Snack," and "Dessert." The bombings were kept secret from the American public. Congress and the media were not told about the bombing raids. Even military records were faked to hide the raids in Cambodia. The records were changed to show that the missions were over Vietnam, not Cambodia.

At first, Operation Menu seemed like a big success. One officer described it as "one of the most effective campaigns of the war."

In mid-April, the Americans began helping the Cambodian army. To maintain secrecy, the Americans gave the Cambodians captured Communist weapons instead of sending American equipment. Americans gave Cambodians about 6,000 captured rifles.

One goal of the bombing was to destroy the Communists' military headquarters. The problem was that no single location existed. Communist forces were scattered all over Cambodia. As the bombs fell, the Communists moved. Instead of moving back into Vietnam, however, the Communist forces moved further west into Cambodia. Within four months, the North Vietnamese Army and Vietcong controlled half of Cambodia.

The Helicopter Gunship

The helicopter was used in new ways in the Vietnam War. It played an important role in almost every U.S. offensive. It was widely used in the Cambodian campaign.

The pilots' favorite gunship was the UH-IC Bell helicopter. It was able to fly more than 100 miles per hour. It was also easier to control than earlier models. The UH-IC had rocket pods on each side. Each pod held seven rockets. It also had two guns inside. Each gun could fire 6,000 rounds of bullets a minute.

The helicopters usually flew in teams of two. They flew at several thousand feet. To attack, the helicopters would dive about 1,500 feet and fire their rockets and guns. As they came out of a dive, they would make a very sharp turn. This maneuver was called "the break." During the break, the guns could not be fired. At this point, the helicopters were almost helpless.

The helicopters were not designed to carry troops or supplies. They were simply meant to be impressive machines that flew around and caused a lot of destruction. Sometimes, the crews would crawl under the helicopters and paint names on them. Many had colorful names, such as "The Sting Ray" and "The Bounty Hunters."

Every night, U.S. crews flew six missions over Cambodia. They would go out, use up all their ammunition, and fly back. Then they would load up again, refuel, and go out again. Finally, at dawn, the missions ended.

The Bombing Exposed

The bombing of Cambodia might have remained secret. But in May 1970 a reporter for *The New York Times* tracked down the story. He reported that while Nixon was putting military pressure on North Vietnam, he was also continuing the peace talks.

Active Learning: Make notes on the bombing of Cambodia for your newspaper article. Your notes should include who ordered the bombings, which targets were attacked, when the bombings took place, and why the bombings took place. What were President Nixon's goals in approving the bombings?

Thinking It Over

1. How did President Nixon hope to achieve "peace with honor"?
2. What was the main effect of Operation Menu?

2 The Invasion of Cambodia

Despite the bombings, the situation in Cambodia worsened. Cambodia asked for more help from the United States. The U.S. government called North Vietnamese actions "a foreign invasion of a neutral country." It claimed that the North Vietnamese and Vietcong had invaded Cambodia.

Speaking to the Nation

On April 30, 1970, President Nixon spoke to the nation. He announced what he called an **incursion** into Cambodia. An incursion is a raid, meaning the soldiers would attack and then withdraw. Nixon said that the operation was not an all-out invasion. American troops would leave after their goals were met. Nixon promised

Once enemy forces are driven out of these sanctuaries and once their military supplies are destroyed, we will withdraw.

In his speech, the President said that he had decided to go to "the heart of the trouble." The goal of the attack was to recapture parts

For months, B-52s, the largest bombers in the U.S. arsenal, dumped tons of bombs on the Ho Chi Minh Trail. But the Communist supply line kept moving.

of Cambodia that were controlled by North Vietnam.

Another objective was to destroy North Vietnamese and Vietcong supplies and troops hidden in the border areas. Nixon said

For five years neither the United States nor South Vietnam has moved against the sanctuaries. We did not want to violate the territory of a neutral country.

The President, however, did not mention in his speech the more than 3,500 American air raids over Cambodia that had taken place since the secret bombing began in March 1969.

Nixon declared that the North Vietnamese must be driven out of Cambodia. He warned that if they were not, all of Cambodia could become a "vast enemy staging area" for future attacks on South Vietnamese and U.S. soldiers.

Two Main Targets

With South Vietnamese forces, American troops began an attack in Cambodia. It involved 32,000 Americans and 48,000 South Vietnamese. The U.S. government did not tell the Cambodian government about the offensive before it began.

The offensive had two major targets. Both targets were in the border area between Cambodia and Vietnam. One target was an area called "Parrot's Beak." It got its name because of its shape. Responsibility for the raid on Parrot's Beak was given to the South Vietnamese. Only American advisers took part in that operation.

The second target was called "Fishhook." It had been a base for the Communists for a long time. About 7,500 Americans and 4,000 South Vietnamese took part in the Fishhook offensive. Helicopters dropped soldiers into the area. They hoped to trap the fleeing Vietcong and North Vietnamese Army. They were also looking for the Communists' headquarters. The headquarters was said to have several thousand workers. The workers lived underground in a huge network of concrete buildings.

Neither the U.S. nor the South Vietnamese forces had much contact with the enemy during the offensive. Most Communist forces had left long before the invasion.

Active Learning: For your article, continue to make notes about the invasion of Cambodia. Remember to ask the "5Ws."

The Invasion: A Balance Sheet

Early in June 1970, President Nixon spoke to the nation again. He called the Cambodian operation the most successful operation of the war. He stated that huge amounts of food and ammunition had been seized. The President declared that the offensive had met all of its goals. He said that the enemy base areas along the border had been destroyed. He told news reporters that the "military balance" of the war had been changed.

However, others believed that the offensive had been far less successful. According to these critics, the invasion had not weakened the Communist forces very much. American forces never found the Communists' secret military headquarters.

The truth is probably somewhere between these two views. There were certainly some short-term gains. The enemy supply system was upset. The Communists lost large amounts of equipment and food. After the invasion, Saigon was in less danger of being attacked. On the other hand, the Americans found few enemy soldiers and seized little major equipment.

There were also losses as a result of the operation. The war had already spread into Cambodia. But it also threatened to extend into Vietnam's other neighbors—Thailand and Laos.

Going to the Source

A Reporter's Diary

Arnaud de Borchgrave was a senior editor at *Newsweek* magazine. During part of the Vietnam War, he was stationed in Cambodia's capitol, Phnom Penh. Below is one week in this reporter's diary.

TUESDAY: The question is whether the North Vietnamese Army will try to take Phnom Penh after the Americans leave. The diplomats here reason that the North Vietnamese must do something spectacular. The Cambodians are bracing for something. "People think the city is under attack. Actually, everything is normal," says a local editorial.

THURSDAY: The Cambodians never seem to know where the NVA [North Vietnamese Army] or VC [Vietcong] are until the shooting starts. . . . The North Vietnamese have been blowing up bridges on all roads leading out of Phnom Penh. By the time the Cambodians reach the scene, the NVA have faded away.

FRIDAY: Visited one of the eighteen refugee camps in Phnom Penh into which some 90,000 Vietnamese residents of Cambodia have been herded. The conditions are bad. Thousands of people in each camp are crowded into small areas with no toilets. The smell is overpowering. These poor people are waiting for boats from Saigon to take them out of Cambodia. But South Vietnam is short of places for the refugees and suspects many are Viet Cong. If they weren't VC before, they certainly must be now.

SATURDAY: The so-called NVA retreat from sanctuaries to the north is nonsense. They are just staying east of the Mekong River. They are putting less pressure on Saigon and the [Mekong] delta. Priorities may even have been switched from Vietnam to Cambodia for the time being. But whatever the Communists lost in the sanctuaries in the way of supplies, has already largely been made up.

SUNDAY: Sirens in Phnom Penh wail for a practice air-raid alert. All cars have to pull over to the curb. . . . It is also the first day of martial law [rule by the military]. There is death by firing squad for anyone in uniform who goes over to the enemy; life imprisonment for anyone involved in corruption; five to twenty years for listening to radio broadcasts from Peking [China], Hanoi [North Vietnam] or the Viet Cong.

MONDAY: Spoke today with a French doctor who spent two weeks among the NVA Seventh Division. The NVA equipment includes many 75mm artillery pieces, 82mm and 60mm mortars, and rocket launchers. From French-owned plantations they seized some 10,000 tons of rice—compared to more than 5,000 tons captured by the U.S. and South Vietnamese forces. . . . It looks as though the NVA are digging in for a long stay in Cambodia.

Adapted from "Cambodia: A Reporter's Diary." *Newsweek*, June 15, 1970.

1. Why does the reporter think that the NVA are digging in for a long stay?
2. Which side, if any, do you think the reporter supports?

The Effect on Cambodia

The Cambodians might be considered the biggest losers. There were now more enemy troops in Cambodia than before the invasion. Much of northeast Cambodia remained under Communist control. The Americans promised to be out of Cambodia by June 30. But the South Vietnamese said that they would stay.

Normal life was no longer possible for Cambodians. People were afraid to travel more than a few miles outside of the cities. Many schools closed. The number of students in school dropped by nearly two-thirds. Most of the hospitals were destroyed. Thousands of refugees fled to cities from battles in the countryside. Cambodia's capital, Phnom Penh, had twice as many people as before the invasion.

Thinking It Over

1. What were the goals of the invasion of Cambodia?
2. What were the results of the Cambodian invasion?

A Good Movie to See

Born on the Fourth of July, MCA Universal Home Video, 1989.

Born on the Fourth of July is the powerful story of Ron Kovic, a real-life Vietnam veteran. Kovic was a high school football star who joined the Marines to fight in Vietnam. Kovic's spine was injured in action, and his legs were paralyzed. The movie follows Kovic through many stages of his life. Eventually, he became active in protesting against the Vietnam War.

3 Protest at Home

The President's decision to invade Cambodia was a shock to Americans. While running for office, Nixon had promised to end the war, but he expanded the war instead.

President Nixon said that he was ready to take the heat for the invasion. He stated that he would rather be a one-term President "than be a two-term President at the cost of seeing America accept the first defeat in its history."

Outrage from Congress

President Nixon and his chief advisers made the decision to invade Cambodia. The President did not consult Congress. His action angered Congress. Members of Congress had not known that the bombings had been taking place for more than a year before the public invasions. Some members believed that Nixon had violated the Constitution by trying to keep the bombings secret.

Congress felt most betrayed by Nixon's ordering an invasion of Cambodia without asking for their permission. Many believed that the President had used more power than the Constitution gave him. They were furious that he had expanded the war beyond Vietnam.

Nixon met with members of Congress to calm the anger building against him. Congress asked Nixon why he had not talked to them before he acted. He said that he did not view the attack as an invasion. He believed that the attack on Cambodia had not violated the country's neutrality.

The President said that the U.S. Constitution made him the commander in chief. Being the commander in chief means that the President commands all the armed forces of the United States. Therefore, he didn't think that it was necessary to get the approval of Congress. Furthermore, he said, for the offensive to be successful, it had to be kept secret.

Nixon made a promise to Congress. He said that all U.S. troops would be out of Cambodia by the end of June 1970.

Congress was not impressed. It threatened to take away some of the President's power to make war. He told them: "I have the constitutional authority to protect American troops in the field." He warned them, "If Congress tries to restrict me, Congress will have to bear the consequences [results]."

Challenging the President

As American troops fought in Vietnam, anti-war feelings were growing in the United States. Some anti-war senators looked for new ways to end the war. They wanted to cut off all funds for American operations in Cambodia after June 30. This proposal was the first time in U.S. history that Congress had tried to limit the President's powers as commander in chief during an armed conflict. The amendment did not pass in the House of Representatives. But it carried a clear warning: The President could no longer do as he pleased in fighting the war.

To show how upset it was with the President, the Senate voted to repeal the Gulf of

During Operation Fishhook, U.S. forces swept into Cambodia looking for a Communist supply base. U.S. troops are shown here next to a large pit holding mortars and rockets left by the fleeing Communists.

Tonkin Resolution. This resolution had been passed in 1964. (See Case Study 2.) It had been used to justify the U.S. involvement in Vietnam. Senator Charles Goodell of New York expressed the views of many senators when he said

I think it's time that the American people recognize that the President doesn't have the power to declare war or make war alone.

A Storm of Protest

The spread of the war into Cambodia led to angry protests in the United States. The protests were strongest among the young. Students at 400 colleges and universities went on strike to protest the war. Campuses became battlefields. There was shooting, rock throwing, and tear gas. One of the worst incidents at the anti-war protests led to the loss of four lives at Kent State University in Ohio. (See Case Study 5.)

Thousands of students marched on Washington. They demanded that Congress take away the President's power to make war. Students who had never before been involved in protests became involved. Most of the protests were peaceful. On May 9, nearly 100,000 protesters came to Washington. They wanted to show the President and Congress that many Americans no longer supported the war effort.

Thinking It Over

1. What was the reaction of Congress to the invasion of Cambodia?
2. What was the reaction on college campuses?

Active Learning: For your news article, describe how many young people reacted to the U.S. invasion in Cambodia.

Case Study Review

Identifying Main Ideas

1. How did both sides in the Vietnam War violate Cambodia's neutrality?
2. Why might Cambodia be considered the biggest loser in the U.S. and South Vietnamese offensive?
3. Why do you think that anti-war protests grew stronger after the invasion of Cambodia?

Working Together

Form a small group. Make a large wall map that shows the countries of North Vietnam, South Vietnam, Laos, Cambodia, and Thailand. Show the Parrot's Beak and Fishhook areas. Indicate the locations of major cities, such as Saigon, Phnom Penh, and Hanoi. Use the map to explain how the Americans hoped to make South Vietnam safer by destroying sanctuaries in Cambodia.

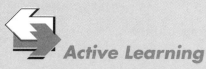 Active Learning

Writing a Newspaper Article Review the notes that you took as you read this case study. Decide on which aspect of the Cambodian invasion you want to focus. Your article should not cover every detail in the case study. But it should give your readers the main ideas and highlights of the event.

Lessons for Today

The ability to think independently is critical to getting involved in civic affairs. Citizens must be able to tell the difference between conflicting statements. During the Vietnam War Americans debated what our country was doing. What does this debate suggest about the need for critical thought in weighing information?

What Might You Have Done?

Imagine that you are an advisor to President Nixon. He is considering sending troops into Cambodia. Might you advise him to keep this action secret or to tell the United States on national television? Explain your choice.

CRITICAL THINKING

Comparing Points of View on Cambodia

Playing a Role

When you role-play, you play the part of another person. You try to think like that person and communicate that person's ideas. Role-playing can help you to understand someone else's point of view.

People often look at historical events from very different points of view. People who feel strongly about an issue are often surprised to find out that a person on the opposite side of an issue can feel just as strongly. One of the most difficult tasks for a critical thinker is to try to put himself or herself "in the other person's shoes." It's difficult to try to look at events from a different point of view.

Form groups of five. Have each student in the group role-play one of the following people:

■ a U.S. soldier going into Cambodia for the first time

■ a member of President Nixon's White House Staff

■ a helicopter pilot flying a gunship over Cambodia

■ a Cambodian citizen living near the border of Vietnam

■ a college student against the war

From the viewpoint of the role that you are playing, think carefully about the following questions. Try to answer the questions as the person you are role-playing would answer them.

1. Describe your overall view of the decision by the United States to bomb and then invade Cambodia.

2. Describe your view of the North Vietnamese and Vietcong sanctuaries in the border areas.

3. Describe your view of expanding the war into Cambodia.

As a group, have a discussion in which you present and compare your individual points of view. Remember that each of you is playing a role. Be sure that everyone has a chance to speak. After the discussion, answer the following questions.

4. In what ways were the views that were presented similar?

5. In what ways were they different?

6. Whose point of view comes closest to your own? Why?

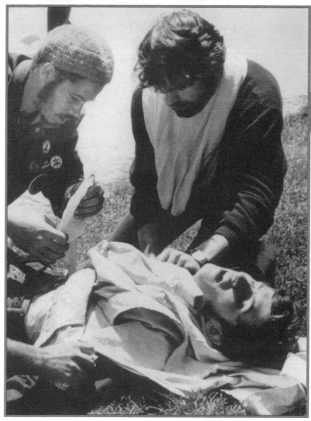

Seriously wounded by gunshots from the National Guard, a Kent State University student lies gasping for air. When the shooting stopped, four students were dead and nine others were wounded.

TRAGEDY AT KENT STATE

CRITICAL QUESTIONS

■ Should the government be allowed to fire on demonstrators who are being abusive?

■ If people believe that a war is wrong, can they do whatever they want to show their opposition?

TERMS TO KNOW

■ Reserve Officer Training Corps (ROTC)

■ corrupt

■ generation gap

■ curfew

■ commons

ACTIVE LEARNING

As you read this case study, take notes on the events that took place at Ohio's Kent State University in May 1970. At the end of the case study, you will hold a "mock trial." After the mock trial, you will decide if anyone committed a crime. If so, who? What punishment, if any, should be carried out?

On Friday morning, May 1, 1970, Tim Butz woke at 6:30 A.M. While eating breakfast, the 22-year-old read the newspaper.

What upset him was the news that President Richard Nixon had ordered U.S. troops into Cambodia.

Butz went to his job. He worked as a librarian at Kent State University in Kent, Ohio. On his way to campus, he saw a lot of graffiti on the walls. The previous night, protesters had spray-painted slogans around the town. Many said, "U.S. Out of Cambodia."

Several students came into the library that morning. They announced that there would be a rally at noon. They planned to bury the U.S. Constitution. One of them said

If our country can launch a war on Cambodia without declaring it, the Constitution is really dead.

Butz was older than most students. He had gone to college after getting out of the Air Force.

He had won many honors fighting in Vietnam. But he was now against any kind of violence. Earlier in the school year, he had joined a group called Vietnam Veterans Against the War.

At 11:45 A.M., the huge bell on campus rang. Butz went to the rally. The crowd was small. About 300 students were there. Butz remembered one of the speeches that a history teacher gave. The teacher explained that President Nixon was going against the Constitution by invading Cambodia. The teacher told the students that they were not responsible for any actions that they might take in protest of the war.

The highlight of the protest was a speech by another Vietnam veteran—Jim Geary, who had won many medals, including the Bronze Star. He said that he was disgusted with how the government was acting. He burned his discharge papers in protest. Butz jumped up beside Geary and announced, "I'm going to burn my papers, too," and he did.

Burning draft cards was a way to protest U.S. involvement in the Vietnam War. Here, a 19-year-old burns his card outside a federal courthouse in Boston, Massachusetts, in 1966.

1 The Anti-War Movement

At universities all over the United States, the invasion of Cambodia led to angry protests. Kent State University was just one of many college campuses that had anti-war protests.

The protests were mostly nonviolent. There were "teach-ins" and "speak-outs" against the war. In these lectures and speeches, people expressed why everyone should oppose the war.

The Protests Turn Violent

After the Cambodian invasion in the spring of 1970, the number and size of the protests increased. Large protests took place on nearly 300 campuses across the country. At some schools, students went on strike. They refused to go to classes. At others, students took over college buildings.

Some of the protests were violent. There were at least 84 bombings. There were also street battles and talk of armed revolution.

One of the protesters' targets was the **Reserve Officer Training Corps** (ROTC), whose programs trained students for the military. Students received college tuition while they took ROTC courses. When the ROTC students finished college, they went into the service as officers. At some colleges, anti-war students burned the buildings that housed the offices of the ROTC.

Other targets were places on campuses where students and professors conducted research for the military. Radical groups thought that by protesting and attacking military research, they could shut down weapons development and production.

Opposing the War

Vietnam was not like previous wars. In World War II, for example, it was easy to pick out the "good guys" from the "bad guys." It was not so easy with Vietnam. The leaders of South Vietnam were sometimes brutal to their own people. Many of the South Vietnamese generals were **corrupt**, or dishonest. Some of these generals stole their soldiers' pay. Some even sold their soldiers' food and supplies to make money for themselves.

Unlike World War II, Americans in Vietnam were often unclear about the reasons for their involvement in the war. The attack on the Gulf of Tonkin was certainly not as severe as the attack on Pearl Harbor. The surprise Japanese attack on Pearl Harbor had forced the United States to enter World War II.

Some protesters viewed the war as a sign of how American society had gone wrong. They saw the problems of race and poverty in the United States. They didn't think that it was right for the United States to police the world when there were so many problems at home.

They also believed that Americans were interfering in Vietnam's internal affairs. In their opinion, U.S. involvement in Vietnam only made life worse for the Vietnamese. The war killed many people. It destroyed much of the country. The spread of the war into Cambodia meant that a new group of people would face destruction.

Others objected to the war for economic reasons. They believed that the United States was wasting its economic resources. In 1967, the United States spent almost $26 billion on the war. Critics pointed out that this money could have been used to improve the quality of life for Americans—instead of destroying life.

Even though their reasons for opposing the war varied, people in the anti-war movement shared a goal. They all wanted to end U.S. involvement in the Vietnam War.

Thinking It Over

1. What were some of the tactics people used in the anti-war movement?
2. Which reason for opposing the war do you think was the strongest? Which one was the weakest? Explain your choices.

2 A Divided Country

Today many people claim that they were against the war from the beginning. However, when President Johnson sent the first combat troops into Vietnam, almost two-thirds of the American public approved.

The American public had many reasons to support the Vietnam War effort. Some believed that all Americans should be patriotic. If the United States was at war, then Americans should support the war. To do anything else would be

Many Americans organized "Support our Boys in Vietnam" parades. They usually were smaller than anti-war protests, but they were just as enthusiastic.

disloyal. Members of veterans groups often felt this way. They wanted to show their support for the young men and women in the service. They were moved by letters, such as this one, written by a soldier.

> Dear Fran,
>
> You asked me if I am bitter. I'm afraid so. Why shouldn't I be? I mean, here I am risking my life fighting communism and there you are with the immature nuts protesting the war.

Many U.S. cities organized "Support Our Boys in Vietnam" parades. Many of the pro-war demonstrations were not well organized. They frequently involved small groups of people saying the Pledge of Allegiance.

Americans who supported the war effort held rallies. They put bumper stickers on their cars. The stickers read, "We Love America," "My Country Right or Wrong," "America—Love It or Leave It" and "Stand Up for Your Country."

To many Americans, the reason for fighting in Vietnam was simple. The Communists were trying to take over South Vietnam. Without help from the United States, South Vietnam would fall. The United States had a responsibility to stop the spread of communism in Asia.

If the United States allowed Communists to take over small countries, then they would try to take over other countries as well. If the United States did not stop them in Cambodia and Vietnam, then the country might end up fighting World War III.

As President Lyndon Johnson said

> If we allow the Communists to win in Vietnam, it will become easier for them to take over other countries in other parts of the world. We will have to fight again some place else. At what cost no one knows.

The Cry for Change

Vietnam and race relations were important issues in the 1960s. But they were not the only issues. During that time, many Americans questioned traditional values.

The United States was the most powerful country in the world. It was richer than it had ever been before. Yet it seemed that the United States had never been so divided.

Many young people in the 1960s rejected the idea that the way to be successful was to go to school, study hard, and get a good job. They rejected almost everything their parents believed in. They wore their hair long. Many dressed in clothing that to adults looked like Halloween costumes. They enjoyed shocking older people with their rough language. They experimented with drugs and played "unusual" and "loud" music.

The music seemed to reflect the rebellion that many young people felt. A record made by Barry McGuire in 1965 was the first of a new wave of songs protesting the war. It was called "Eve of Destruction." A song that spoke about the need for change, "Blowin' in the Wind," written by Bob Dylan, became the theme song for many young people. The Byrds; the Rolling Stones; The Doors; The Who; and Crosby, Stills, and Nash wrote and sang songs protesting the war.

The Generation Gap

On one side were many young Americans. They were the sons and daughters of the middle class. They dressed "funny" and wore their hair long. Many no longer believed in the traditional goals of American life. They were called "hippies" or "flower children." They believed in "doing your own thing."

On the other side were many parents. Many of them had lived through the Great Depression and World War II. Their dream had been to have a well-paying job and a home of their own. They wanted their children to have everything that they did not have when they were growing up.

The two groups did not seem to have much in common. Because each group belonged to a different generation, these differences were called the **generation gap**.

The Vietnam War added to the gap. Many members of the older generation supported the war. Many young people opposed it. Communication broke down between the two groups. Many families suffered the same split that the United States seemed to be experiencing.

Thinking It Over

1. What issues—other than Vietnam—divided the United States in the 1960s?
2. Which group tended to support the Vietnam War? Why?

A Good Book to Read

Hell No, We Won't Go, by Sherry Gottlieb. New York: Viking Press, 1991.

This is the story of several American anti-war protesters. Some of these stories are told by well-known people. Some are told by ordinary people. Their stories help readers understand why Americans were so divided over Vietnam.

3 Shootings at Kent State

Kent is a small city in northeastern Ohio. It is best known for its university, Kent State. In 1970, Kent State had not yet faced the violent protests that other colleges had experienced. Yet, it had many students who believed that the war in Vietnam was wrong. The burying of the Constitution began the chain of events at the university that would change the country.

As the sun set on May 1, 1970, a crowd began to gather on Water Street, which was in the center of Kent, Ohio. The street attracted a lot of college students. It was also popular with many people who did not attend the college. On the night of May 1, a number of runaways, motorcycle gangs, and numerous students were on the street.

At 10:15 P.M., someone started throwing firecrackers. The firecrackers excited the crowd. Someone tossed a bottle at a passing car. A restaurant worker called the police. A patrol car arrived only to be hit with another bottle. The crowd got rougher. Some girls yelled at passing cars: "Pigs off the street! We won't go to Cambodia!"

After 11 P.M., serious trouble began. The crowd formed a human-chain barricade and stopped traffic along Water Street. Young people started dumping trash cans in the middle of the street. Some set them on fire.

Near midnight, the crowd paraded through the center of town. People threw rocks at stores and homes and broke about 50 windows.

Active Learning: In preparation for your mock trial, think about the answers to the following questions. How do you feel about the students burying the U.S. Constitution? How do you feel about the other activities that took place after the students found out about the Cambodian invasion? Did the young people break the law? Or were they just expressing themselves in legal ways?

As tear gas swells around them, demonstrators at Kent State University jeer at National Guard troops. The demonstrators soon began to throw rocks and bits of concrete. Moments later, the Guard fired into the crowd, killing four students.

Enter the National Guard

The next day, the mayor of Kent went to his office, even though it was Saturday. He was angry and concerned. All morning, there had been rumors of more trouble. He knew that Kent's 21 police officers would not be enough if trouble started. He decided to ask the governor of Ohio to call in the National Guard. The National Guard is made up of citizens who can be called to service by the state in times of emergency.

Around 7:30 that night, another large crowd gathered in downtown Kent. It marched toward the ROTC building yelling, "Down with ROTC!" Soon, there were about 2,000 students gathered near the building. The crowd broke down the main door. Someone in the crowd threw railroad flares through a broken window. Within a few minutes, the ROTC building burst into flames.

As the building burned, the protesters cheered and yelled: "Burn, baby, burn!" The thick, black smoke could be seen from City Hall. By 10:30 P.M., the building was destroyed.

By that time, the National Guard troops had arrived in Kent. The mayor asked the troops to help protect downtown Kent. As the troops moved in, some protesters tossed rocks at them.

Suddenly, the protesters heard a rumbling. Then they saw what they thought was a tank. It was followed by two troop carriers filled with National Guardsmen. Then came a line of jeeps. Finally, there were some big trucks. As the troops entered the campus, a protester said, "My God, they've got guns."

Profiling the National Guard Troops

The National Guard troops on duty at Kent State spent that night at a local elementary school. Most of the men were in their 20s. They were not professional soldiers. They all had civilian jobs. Many had joined the National Guard to make a little extra money.

They were proud of their outfit and their training. The Ohio National Guard had been called out many times to stop riots. It had also fought in most of the U.S. wars overseas. Some of the soldiers attended Kent State and knew many of the students.

Sunday morning began calmly. Kent was filled with students and sightseers. They were looking at the burned remains of the ROTC building. Students talked quietly as they wandered around. There was no hint of the violence of the previous two nights.

One of the guards talked with several students to try to lessen the tension. This tactic seemed to work well. A famous picture shows a student placing a flower in the muzzle of one of the guard's guns.

The town of Kent was under a **curfew**. A curfew is an order to be at home during certain hours. As night came, most people went home. For a while, everything was quiet.

"Someone Is Going to Get Killed"

At about 7 P.M., a small crowd gathered on campus. They chanted anti-war slogans. An informal march started. A National Guard officer shouted through a bullhorn, "You are breaking the law. If you continue to demonstrate you will be arrested." The crowd ignored him.

A group of the marchers decided to march into the city of Kent. They sang and cheered as they walked to Main Street.

The students decided to sit in the middle of the street. The scene grew ugly. All the goodwill of the morning was quickly forgotten. Some students cursed at the National Guard troops. One guardsman warned the students: "If this keeps up, somebody's going to get killed."

As the crowd grew larger, the students became bolder. They moved closer and closer to the guard troops. One guard remembered his feelings at the time. He said, "I was sure we'd be rushed. I was afraid of what might happen if we were."

At 11 P.M., the troops moved on the crowd. They chased after the students. But as the students ran, they pounded the guards with

Going to the Source

Ohio's Governor Reacts to the Shootings

James Rhodes was the governor of Ohio at the time of the protests at Kent State University. At a press conference on May 3, 1970, he reacted to the protests in the following way.

The scene here that the city of Kent is facing is probably the most vicious form of campus violence yet carried on by groups and their allies in the state of Ohio. Now it is not just a problem for the colleges of Ohio. This is now the problem for the whole state of Ohio. Now we're going to put a stop to this, for this reason. The same group that we're dealing with here today, and there's three or four of them, they only have one thing in mind. That is to destroy higher education in Ohio.

Last night I think we saw all forms of violence. It was the worst. And when they start taking over communities, that is when we're going to use every weapon of the law-enforcement agencies of Ohio to drive them out of Kent. We have these same groups going from one campus to the other, and they use the universities that are supported by the taxpayers of Ohio as a sanctuary. They make definite plans of burning, destroying, and throwing rocks at police at the National Guard and the Highway Patrol. . . . They're worse than the Communist element. They are worse than night riders and Ku Klux Klan. They're the worst type of people that we harbor in America.

It's over within Ohio. I think that we're up against the strongest, well-trained, militant revolutionary group that has ever assembled in America. We are going to end the problem. We're not going to treat the symptom.

From Joseph Kelner, *The Kent State Coverup* (New York: Harper, 1980), p. 165.

1. Who did Governor Rhodes say had caused the problem?

2. Why do you think that Governor Rhodes compared the protesters to "the Communist element" and the Ku Klux Klan?

3. What did Governor Rhodes mean when he said: "We are going to end the problem. We're not going to treat the symptom"?

rocks. Guards injured seven students with bayonets. Most of the injuries were not serious enough to require hospital care. The rest of the students pulled back. The demonstrations were over for that night.

Monday Turns Bloody

At 11 the next morning, students began collecting on the **commons**, a large, open area in the center of the campus. It was usual for students to gather on the commons as they went to and from their classes.

Many of the students had been away during the weekend. They did not know that the rally scheduled for noon that day had been forbidden by the governor of Ohio.

The general in charge of the National Guard was worried. He saw the large number of students on the commons. The crowd kept getting larger. The general ordered the guard troops to break up the crowd. He said

If you have not already done so, load and lock. Prepare for gas attack. Prepare to move out.

Just before noon, the 113 guard troops present prepared to scatter the crowd. No one knows just how many students were involved. Many were just curious and interested in what was going on. The number of students on the commons itself was close to 1,000. Several thousand others watched from farther away.

The troops fired tear gas into the crowd. Some students picked up the tear gas cans and threw them back. They threw rocks and hunks of concrete and cursed the guards.

At about 12:15 P.M., the troops were ordered to withdraw. They were angry and may have felt

Their faces covered by gas masks, Ohio National Guard troops fire tear gas into the crowd at Kent State. Most of the troopers were young men with civilian jobs. They were not trained to restrain an angry mob without using violence.

threatened. But many of the guards were tired of the way the students had been acting. Perhaps some were afraid.

Suddenly, one group of guards turned around and lowered their rifles to a firing position. A single shot was fired, followed by a quick series of other shots. The shooting lasted only 13 seconds. Twenty-eight guard troops fired their weapons. Most fired into the air. Some fired right into the crowd. When the shooting stopped, 13 students had been shot. Four were dead.

Thinking It Over

1. Why was the National Guard called out by the governor of Ohio?
2. Did the National Guard troops have a good reason to fire upon the students? Why or why not?

Active Learning: In the mock trial, you will be required to make judgments. Practice this skill by making a judgment about the National Guard troops. Why did they fire into the crowd? By firing at the students, were they committing a crime? Were their commanding officers at fault? Should anyone have been arrested?

4 After the Firing

President Richard Nixon learned about the shootings about an hour later. He was stunned. An aide to Nixon remembered his saying

The National Guard themselves are a bunch of scared kids with guns. With a mob hurling rocks at a bunch of scared kids with guns, you shouldn't be surprised if some of the guns go off.

On college campuses, the reaction was swift. Student protests spread to several hundred colleges. College faculties joined in protesting the Cambodian invasion and the Kent State shootings. Protests were held at more than 1,000 colleges. More than 536 campuses were shut down. As many as half of the nation's college students were involved in anti-war protests.

The violence and attacks on ROTC buildings continued after the shootings. At more than 100 schools, National Guard troops were called to maintain order.

Public Opinion Changes

Previously, labor unions had been strong supporters of the war effort. Then some unions began to criticize it. On May 7, 1970, one large union called for the United States to withdraw from Vietnam. More workers joined in anti-war protests.

The Role of the Media

After the shootings at Kent State, newspapers and television continued their criticism of the U.S. role in Vietnam. On the day of the Kent State deaths, television networks kept replaying scenes from the tragedy.

Many people identified with the so-called "Kent Four" who were killed. Two of the victims were 19 years old. The other two were 20. One of the students who died was Allison Krause, who had placed a flower in a trooper's rifle the previous day. Another student was Bill Shroeder. He was called an "all-American" boy and was in his second year of ROTC training. Sandy Scheuer was remembered as a happy girl who only wanted to make others happy. Jeff Miller tied back his long hair with a headband. He was

Led by a mother whose son had died in the fighting in Vietnam, anti-war demonstrators protest through the streets of Berkeley, California, in 1966.

an easy-going kid who did pretty much what his friends did.

The media showed pictures of the dead students from their old high school yearbooks. Many Americans felt sorrow for the students' families. Allison Krause's father appeared on television. He asked whether it was a crime to disagree with the government. Was this a reason for killing his daughter?

In the months that followed the shootings, the American people saw huge anti-war protests on television. Hundreds of thousands of Americans came to Washington to try to convince Congress to end the war. During one moving moment, some Vietnam veterans threw their medals onto the steps of the Capitol to show their anger at the government.

All the media coverage had a strong effect on the American public. Public opinion polls showed that 61 percent of Americans believed that the war was a mistake.

On the other hand, many Americans were angry with the media. They believed that the media was using the Kent State shootings for its own selfish ends. They believed that the National Guard troops had been provoked by the demonstrators.

The Protests Affect U.S. Policy

The huge protests in the United States forced a change in policy. President Nixon announced a new policy that he called "Vietnamization." Nixon stated that the responsibility for fighting the war would fall on South Vietnam. Of course, the United States would continue to supply the South Vietnamese army. It would supply advisers and equipment. American bombers would continue air support. But most of the burden of the war would be on the South Vietnamese.

Thinking It Over

1. What effect did the Kent State shootings have on U.S. society?
2. How did newspapers and magazines shape public opinion?

Case Study Review

Identifying Main Ideas

1. What happened at Kent State University in early May 1970?
2. How did President Nixon respond to the Kent State shootings?
3. How did the events at Kent State affect public opinion about the war?

Working Together

Form a small group. Discuss the teacher's comment that the students were not responsible for any actions that they took to protest the Cambodian invasion. Pick a slip out of a hat to decide whether you will support the teacher's view or oppose it. Hold a debate, then have the class decide which group "won" the debate.

Active Learning

Conducting a Mock Trial Review the notes that you took as you read this case study. As a class, decide if a crime or crimes were committed. If so, who committed the crimes? National Guard troops? their officers? students who held violent protests?

Appoint students to play the parts of judge, lawyers, the accused, and witnesses. Then conduct the mock trial. List the charges. The lawyers should ask questions of the witnesses and the accused. The witnesses must answer honestly. All the students who are not involved in the trial should act as the jury. They should decide whether the accused are guilty or innocent. If guilty, what should the punishment be?

Lessons for Today

Marching in protests, flag burning, and burying the U.S. Constitution were all forms of protest during the Vietnam War. According to the Constitution, citizens have the right to criticize the government. However, do protesters have the right to break the law? Should there be limits on protests against the government? Can there be a balance between individual freedom and the need to obey the law?

What Might You Have Done?

Imagine that you are a young college student in 1970. Some of your classmates are breaking the law by burning their draft cards and attacking the police. Write a statement revealing how you feel about the war and the actions of the protesters.

Examining Assumptions

Assumptions can be correct or incorrect. They often lead to certain kinds of behavior or consequences. Someone who assumes that you like country-and-western music may give you a recording of that music. Some assumptions are not so pleasant. You might assume that your friends will remember your birthday and therefore you don't remind them of the date. You might assume that a sales clerk will always give correct change and therefore you don't count your change right away.

What experiences have you had with assumptions? Copy the graphic organizer below on a separate piece of paper and use it to describe correct and incorrect assumptions that you have made or that someone else has made. Choose a person or idea about which assumptions were made. Write the name of the person or idea in the central oval. Then write the assumptions in the labeled boxes.

Assumptions may be right or wrong. They also may be obvious or not so obvious. Suppose that an advertisement states, "We've dropped the price of a Zandar computer to $699. Now everyone can own one." The two assumptions behind this advertisement are that everyone has $699 to spend on a Zandar computer and that everyone wants to buy a computer.

When considering a writer's or speaker's ideas, critical thinkers examine the assumptions behind them. Critical thinkers ask whether these assumptions are true. If not, the writer's or speaker's reasoning may be faulty.

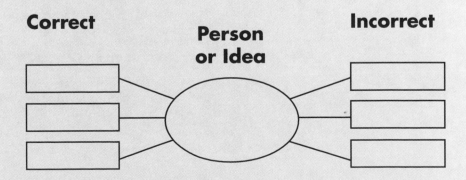

The Language of Thinking

People may use facts or opinions to make assumptions. A fact is something that is known to be true. Facts can be proven. An opinion is a belief based on what someone thinks, not on something that can be proven. Critical thinkers know that facts are more reliable than opinions.

People often make assumptions about other people. Some assumptions are generous. Some are harmful. Harmful assumptions can lead to harmful actions against a person or group. For example, a shopkeeper might assume that all teenagers are shoplifters. He might show this suspicion by following teenagers around or watching them very closely. He might treat teenagers like criminals, based on a harmful assumption.

When you examine or evaluate assumptions, you look for the truth. You ask questions that help you know what is real or factual. Those questions should include the following:

- What are the facts?
- What are the assumptions?
- What actions were taken based on these assumptions?
- How can inaccurate assumptions be corrected?
- How can correct assumptions be clarified?

Turn to the text on page 67 that deals with the generation gap. Using your own ideas, respond to the questions below.

1. What values and beliefs did many people in the older generation share?

2. What values and beliefs did many young people share?

3. What assumptions did many older people make about the young people?

4. What assumptions did many young people make about older people?

5. Do you believe that these assumptions were always right? Explain your answer.

6. Can you tell what a person believes just by the way he or she dresses and acts?

7. How can inaccurate assumptions lead to misunderstandings and conflict?

When buddies were wounded in combat, racial differences evaporated. Soldiers did not think about the color of one another's skin. They thought only of the safety of the unit.

A MULTICULTURAL FIGHTING FORCE

CRITICAL QUESTIONS

■ Why did American minorities play a huge role in the Vietnam War?

■ What were the experiences of women, African Americans, Native Americans, and Latinos in Vietnam?

TERMS TO KNOW

■ volunteer

■ symbol

■ interpreter

ACTIVE LEARNING

After you have read this case study, you will be asked to draw a mural honoring the multicultural fighting forces that served in Vietnam. As you read, think about the images that you will add to your mural.

About 11,000 American women served on active military duty in Vietnam. Most **volunteered** to go to Vietnam. A volunteer is someone who agrees to go to war without being drafted. Pinkie Hauser was one of the many women volunteers.

Hauser volunteered for duty in Vietnam in 1968. She was sent there in September 1969. She remembered the long flight from the United States. There were about 300 male GIs and only two women on the airplane. When she arrived in Vietnam, she asked herself the question that most new arrivals asked, "What am I doing here?"

The most difficult night she had when she first arrived in the country was about one week into her stay. She was lying in bed when suddenly the bed started moving. She jumped up and asked, "What's going on?" Her roommate replied, "The B-52s are bombing."

Hauser was with the Army Engineer Corps. Her work was secret. Even today, although the war is over, she will not talk about her work. All that she will say is that she would go out in the field with the unit's officers. She had to wear a bulletproof vest. She weighed only about 90 pounds. It seemed to Hauser as though the vest that she wore weighed almost as much as she did.

Sometimes, after work, she would visit wounded soldiers. "Some of the things that I saw will stick in my mind as long as I live," she said.

She remembers seeing GIs so badly injured that she could not recognize any of their features. Many soldiers had missing arms and legs. Hauser remembered that in the 13 months that she was in Vietnam, she never got used to the smell of the wounded and dying solders.

Two million American men were drafted to fight in Vietnam. Here, a group of young men from western Pennsylvania are sworn into the U.S. Army. Most of them would soon be off to Vietnam.

1 Facing the Draft

At the beginning, most of the men and women who served in Vietnam were volunteers. But soon more and more combat troops were needed. The military had to increase its ranks in another way. That way was the draft.

Raising an Army

During the Vietnam War, men between the ages of 18 and 35 were required to register for the draft. At first, most men thought that their chances of being drafted were low. In the early years of American involvement in Vietnam, the government drafted only about 7,000 men between the ages of 18 and 26 each month. But the need for soldiers kept growing. Soon, 50,000 men were being called for action each month, including men up to 35 years old.

In the end, two million men were drafted during the Vietnam War. By 1970, draftees made up 70 percent of the combat soldiers. Forty-three percent of the combat soldiers killed in Vietnam were draftees.

The Deferment System

Men who were eligible to be drafted could ask to be deferred. Sometimes their deferment was only temporary; other times they would never have to go into military service.

A man could be deferred because he had an important job and could not be easily replaced. At the time, the country needed engineers, teachers, and police officers. Therefore, men in these occupations could be deferred, if they chose.

The main reason that young men were deferred was that they were attending college. As long as a young man kept up his grades, he could be deferred. Referring to the new grading system, many college students said: "A, B, C, D, Nam."

Bearing the Burden of War

African Americans and other minorities were more likely to be drafted than whites. Although deferments were available to everyone, minorities were not as likely to be deferred because many did not have the money to attend college.

Minorities did more than their share of the fighting and dying in Vietnam. This fact had to do largely with their being poor. Most combat soldiers came from low-income homes. High school dropouts had a 70 percent chance of going to Vietnam. This chance was nearly twice as high as the rate for college graduates.

Lottery

Many Americans criticized the deferment system because it seemed unfair to minorities. In response to the criticism, a lottery system was introduced in 1969. The new system made the draft more impartial. In other words, everyone—rich and poor alike—had an equal chance of being drafted. It also ended all college deferments.

Under the lottery system, the 366 possible days of the year were written on individual

A Good Book to Read

Bloods: An Oral History of the Vietnam War, by Wallace Terry. New York: Random House, 1984.

Wallace Terry interviewed 20 African American veterans of Vietnam. African Americans fought two wars in Vietnam. As "grunts," they fought the Vietcong and the North Vietnamese. But as African Americans, they also fought prejudice and racism. Their stories are honest and moving.

cards. The cards were drawn one at a time from a drum. A man whose birthday fell on the date shown on the first card drawn would be among the first ones drafted. A man whose birthday fell on one of the last cards drawn would most likely not be drafted that year.

Thinking It Over

1. What was a deferment?
2. For what reasons were some men deferred from military service?

Active Learning: As you plan your mural, think about whether you want to show only people. You may also want to use **symbols**. A symbol is a picture that stands for something else. For example, a dove can be a symbol of peace. An exploding bomb could be a symbol of war.

2 Three Stories of Heroism

Vietnam war heroes came from big cities and from small towns. A few enlisted; many were drafted. Some were officers; others were grunts. Some served on the front lines; others served as support troops. Some drove the trucks that supplied the troops; others cooked the meals.

Many of the men and women who served in Vietnam performed heroic acts. The experiences of the following three soldiers serve as examples of those heroic deeds.

Luther Benton, Hospital Corpsman

Luther Benton did not have to go to Vietnam; he volunteered. As the only son in his family, he could have asked to be assigned somewhere else. But he wanted to serve his country in Vietnam.

Benton was stationed at a South Vietnamese military hospital as a medical supply adviser. He spent a year helping to improve conditions at the hospital. As the medical supply adviser for the area, Benton also issued medical supplies to the South Vietnamese.

August 27, 1967 was a day that Benton would never forget. At about 2 A.M., the Vietcong attacked the hospital compound where he

African Americans contributed more than their share to the war effort. Here, medic James Sims braves fire to tend to a wounded comrade outside Tay Ninh in 1967.

worked. People were running everywhere. The Vietcong quickly slipped inside the compound. When they got close to his bunker, Benton picked up a rifle that he had hidden away and started shooting.

Benton fought for his life. He and another soldier found boxes of grenades. They just pulled the pins and threw them. Suddenly, a rocket hit the ground nearby. It blew both men into the air. The blast was so strong that all the fillings in Benton's teeth were blown out. After he landed, he just picked up his weapon and started firing again. He did not stop fighting until dawn. Benton won the Bronze Star for his actions.

Emmanuel H. Holloman, Interpreter

Emmanuel Holloman went to Vietnam in 1966. The army sent him to language school to learn Vietnamese. One of Holloman's military duties was to act as an **interpreter**. An interpreter is someone who translates one foreign language into another language.

Holloman's other responsibility was to give U.S. money to the families of Vietnamese who were killed or to families whose homes were destroyed. These casualties occurred often. The families were not given much money. They received about $40 from the U.S. government for a dead relative. They received about $9 for a destroyed home. Holloman always tried to give the families a little more money.

Holloman helped to rebuild homes that were destroyed. Sometimes he collected extra food and took it to an orphanage or gave it to refugees. He formed close relationships with the people. When Vietnamese were hurt, he visited them. He also often ate meals with a family.

Holloman believed that African Americans got along better with the Vietnamese than whites. Maybe, he thought, it was because they knew how difficult life was for the Vietnamese. According to Holloman

I could understand poverty. I have five brothers and three sisters. My mother works

in an old folks' home. My father works in a garage.

Holloman fell in love with a South Vietnamese woman. He was sent home before the paperwork could be completed that would allow him to marry his girlfriend. He returned to Vietnam in 1971 and found her. He tried to get her out again but failed. After the Communists took over in 1975, he never heard from her again.

Roy P. Benavidez, Special Forces

"Get us out of here! For God's sake, get us out!" The voice over the radio was desperate. A Special Forces unit had come under fire from a much larger North Vietnamese force. The team leader was calling for a helicopter to take him and his men out.

Sergeant Roy Benavidez rushed to the helicopter pad. He jumped into a helicopter. He told the surprised pilot, "I'm going with you." The enemy fire was intense. Benavidez ordered the pilot to drop him off as close to the men as he could. The helicopter could not drop lower than 10 feet from the ground. Roy crossed himself and jumped. The enemy fired at him. He felt bullets cut across his legs and face, but he kept going.

Reaching the team, Benavidez found four men dead. He saw eight others wounded. The helicopter touched down, but it was disabled before it could rescue the men. Benavidez pulled out two of the helicopter's crew before he was shot in the back by a sniper.

Still Benavidez did not give up. He gave the men water and ammunition even though he was bleeding from bullet wounds all over his body. Blood from his head wounds made it difficult for him to see.

Benavidez and the others were on the ground for eight hours. When a helicopter finally got close enough to land, Benavidez helped to load the wounded and dead. Finally, he was pulled aboard. He collapsed near a pile of bodies.

At the base, a doctor thought that Benavidez was dead. He prepared a body bag for him. Unable to move or speak, Benavidez spit into the surprised doctor's face to let the doctor know that he was alive. He was rushed to a Saigon hospital. Everyone assumed that Benavidez would die, but he slowly recovered.

His commanding officer asked the Army to give Benavidez the Medal of Honor. This medal is the nation's highest honor for bravery. But there were problems. Army rules required at least two eyewitnesses to his heroism. But most of the men from the Special Forces unit had died.

In 1980, after reading a newspaper story about Benavidez's campaign for the medal, the only surviving member of the team spoke out. He thought that Benavidez had been killed. Finally, on February 24, 1981, President Ronald Reagan presented Roy Benavidez with the Medal of Honor. He was the last living man to receive the Medal of Honor for bravery in the Vietnam War.

Thinking It Over

1. Why did the Army need an interpreter, such as Emmanuel Holloman?
2. Why did Roy Benavidez not receive his Medal of Honor immediately?

Active Learning: You might want to note some of the acts of bravery discussed in this case study so that you'll remember to include them in your mural.

3 Minorities and the War

According to the 1980 Census, 344,500 Latino men served in Vietnam. Many fought on the front lines. The percentage of Latinos wounded and killed was high. Several Latinos were awarded the Medal of Honor. As you have learned, the last living person awarded the Medal of Honor for service in Vietnam was Staff Sergeant Roy P. Benavidez. The first POW of the war was Lieutenant Commander Everett Alvarez Jr., who was Latino. (See Case Study 2.)

Native Americans and the War

Native American men have fought in every American war. They played a key role in World War II. Large numbers of men were recruited from reservations across the country for the war effort. Several Native American languages were used as codes during the war. The Navajo code talkers developed a code that the Japanese were unable to decipher.

According to the U.S. Census, there are 160,000 living Native American veterans. This number represents about 10 percent of all living Native Americans. Over 42,000 Native Americans were stationed in Southeast Asia during the Vietnam War. In 1972, between 20,000 and 30,000 Native Americans volunteered to serve in Vietnam.

Like other minorities, Native Americans were often poor and faced racial prejudice. They had few chances to get decent jobs outside of the military. Robert Emery, a Native American from Nebraska, recalled that it was always a struggle to stay ahead. He and his two brothers went into the service. However, because of the reactions against Vietnam veterans, the war did not give Native Americans a chance to rise above the poverty level. After the war, many Native American Vietnam veterans became leaders of such militant Indian rights organizations as the American Indian Movement (AIM).

Going to the Source

A Poem About Vietnam

Some people find that they can best express how they feel in poetry. The following poem was inspired by the Vietnam War. It is from a collection by W.D. Ehrhart called *To Those Who Have Gone Home Tired.*

Guerrilla War

It's practically impossible
to tell civilians
from the Vietcong.

Nobody wears uniforms.
They all talk
the same language
(and you couldn't understand them
even if they didn't).

They tape grenades
inside their clothes,
and carry satchel charges
in their market baskets.

Even their women fight;
and young boys,
and girls.

It's practically impossible to tell civilians
from the Vietcong.
After awhile
you quit trying.

    —W.D. Ehrhart

From W.D. Ehrhart, *To Those Who Have Gone Home Tired*
(New York: Thunder's Mouth Press Inc., 1984), p. 12.

1. What do you think is the main idea of W.D. Ehrhart's poem?
2. What do you think the last two lines of this poem suggest?

African Americans in Vietnam

The attitudes of many African American soldiers reflected what was happening at home. African Americans who were sent to Vietnam had lived through the civil rights movement. They had strong opinions about the unfairness of the draft. They were not willing to put up with racism at home or in Vietnam.

When young African Americans and other minority troops were off duty, they would often get together. They would sit around, talking about anything and everything except the war.

Military leaders sent a committee to Vietnam in 1969 to check on race relations. It reported that race relations were tense and advised that some steps be taken immediately.

The Defense Department issued orders to eliminate unfair treatment of minorities. The number of African Americans on the front lines was reduced. Before 1969, African Americans made up almost 40 percent of the combat troops in Vietnam. By the end of the war, the African American percentage of total battlefield deaths was 12 percent. This percentage is about equal to that of African Americans in the U.S. population.

Race Relations on the Front Lines

Race relations were best on the front lines of combat. The soldiers in combat worked together, lived together—and died together. Race was not important when people depended on each other for their lives. The only thing that was important was how quickly they responded in combat.

Stephen Howard was an African American soldier. His first white friend was a fellow soldier in Vietnam. Howard described his white friend as a "redneck" from Georgia. He called his friend "Rosey." The two soldiers discovered that they had a lot in common. Rosey was the son of a sharecropper. There were times when his family was so poor that they did not have any food. Howard also grew up in a poor family.

Most soldiers who served on the front lines remember friendships between people of all races. One white soldier recalled the day his African American buddy was shipped out

He gave me his picture and when he got on the truck to leave, he wouldn't let go of my hand.

Thinking It Over

1. How did soldiers of various ethnic backgrounds get along on the front lines?
2. Why do you think that soldiers showed less prejudice than people who were not soldiers?

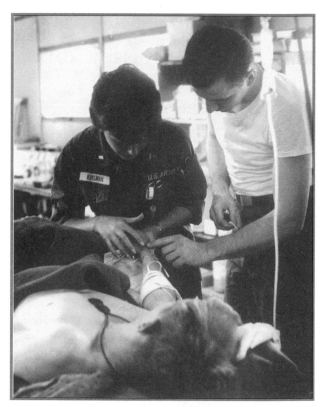

Working under harsh battlefield conditions, thousands of U.S. Army nurses tended to the wounded and injured. Here, a nurse prepares a wounded soldier to receive blood.

Women in War

Women have participated in every war, but their role was seldom recognized. Part of the reason for not recognizing them is that only a small number of women have been combat soldiers. However, this does not mean that women were not involved in the war effort in a variety of ways.

In U.S. history, women were very much involved in the two wars fought on U.S. soil. During the American Revolution, women manufactured gunpowder used by U.S. forces. In the Civil War, women produced much of the clothing, food, and medical supplies. In both wars, women nursed the injured.

World War I was the first war in which American women officially served in the military. More than 25,000 women crossed the ocean to take care of the war's victims.

During World War II, American women joined the armed forces for the first time. By 1944, more than 100,000 women were in the military services.

Women Civilians in Vietnam

About 55,000 American women served in Vietnam. Most of the women were civilians. Many worked for the American Red Cross. They served as an important communication link between the soldiers and their families.

Women also supported the soldiers in a variety of ways. They ran base camp centers where the soldiers could get together, play cards, shoot pool, or just talk. Civilian women also worked as flight attendants on the planes that flew Americans in and out of Vietnam.

Micki Voisard was a civilian who served in Vietnam. On an average tour of one to two weeks, she would see about 1,200 to 1,500 young men. Voisard later said that she was like two different people in Vietnam. "I had to be a cheerleader for the guys going over." Then, on the way home, she had to explain to the men that home was not the same as they had left it and that they might not fit in right away.

During the Vietnam War, the Armed Forces Radio hired its first woman DJ. Her name was Chris Noel. "Hi, Luv" was the opening for her show, called "A Date with Chris." During her hour-long program, Noel played Top 40 songs. To many of the men in Vietnam, Noel was a substitute girlfriend.

Women in the Military in Vietnam

Most of the women who served in Vietnam, though, were nurses. There was a great need for nurses. So all the branches of the service recruited women.

Most of the nurses were not prepared for Vietnam. More than half had less than two years of nursing experience before going to Vietnam. Even experienced nurses were not prepared for what they saw.

Leslie McClusky was a nurse who joined the military. She joined because she "wanted to grow up." She was sent to a camp in the northern part of South Vietnam.

While in Vietnam, she grew up fast. The first wounded person she saw was a boy whose leg had been blown off. There were many wounded soldiers brought into the hospital at the same time. After a while, she said, she became numb to the horror.

Ann Polas was just 19 years old and fresh out of nursing school when she joined the Army. On her flight to Vietnam, she noticed that the plane did not make a long, gradual descent when it was time to land. It just dropped. There were no lights on the plane. She found out that the reason for the strange landing was to avoid being shot down.

Polas said that one of the biggest problems she faced as a nurse in Vietnam was GIs on drugs. The most common drug problem for the soldiers was heroin. Many of her patients were shooting it, even though they were injured or wounded. The situation was so bad that one of

Americans serving in Vietnam came from all ethnic and income groups. This sea of faces was part of a U.S. battalion that is enjoying a performance of a Broadway show near the city of An Khe in 1965.

the hospital bays, or wings, was used just for addicted patients.

Not all of the women in the military were nurses. More than 1,300 military women worked outside the medical field. As you have learned, Pinkie Hauser did secret work with the Army Engineer Corps. Many women worked as clerks on large bases. Some were air traffic controllers and mapmakers. Many women had security clearances, which let them work on decoding secret messages.

Yet despite their many contributions to the war effort, the women who served in Vietnam have received little recognition. There are only a few books about the important roles that women played. Many movies have been made about the war. However, the only women in them are usually Vietnamese.

Thinking It Over

1. a) In what previous American wars did women serve? (b) In what positions did they serve?
2. List at least three roles that American women played in Vietnam.

Active Learning: Be sure that your mural reflects the many important roles, both civilian and military, that women played in the war.

Case Study Review

Identifying Main Ideas

1. Why did the United States draft men to fight in Vietnam?
2. How did the war change the ways in which African Americans and whites related to each other?
3. What job did most of the military women in Vietnam hold?

Working Together

Form a small group. Then prepare a brief script on "The Life of an African American Soldier in Vietnam," "The Life of a Latino Soldier in Vietnam," "The Life of a Native American Soldier in Vietnam," or "The Life of an American Woman in Vietnam." The script should run no longer than 15 minutes. Reread the relevant portions of this case study in order to make your script realistic.

 ## Active Learning

Creating a Mural Review your ideas for the mural. Now decide what form your mural will take. Sketch it out. When your mural is complete, show it to the class and describe what you have drawn. Explain why you chose to include what you did. The class should provide feedback on the ideas and events that you have chosen.

Lessons for Today

General Colin Powell was one of the highest-ranking officers in the U.S. Army. During the Persian Gulf War of 1991, he was Chairman of the Joint Chiefs of Staff. This position is the highest American military office that a person can hold. General Powell served as an officer in Vietnam. What does General Powell's success say about opportunities for African Americans in the armed forces? Explain your answer.

What Might You Have Done?

Imagine that you are a college student in 1967 when you are drafted. One of your friends, who is also a college student, has received a deferment. Another friend is serving in Vietnam. What might you do? Might you request a deferment until you graduate from college? Or might you accept being drafted? Before you answer these questions, keep in mind that there were numerous viewpoints about the war and American involvement in the war effort.

CRITICAL THINKING

Noting Similarities and Differences

The words *compare* and *contrast* often appear in the textbooks that you use. You are often asked to complete exercises that ask how one person's ideas about something are similar to or different from another person's ideas.

Critical thinkers understand that ideas that seem alike on the surface are often quite different. On the other hand, ideas that seem opposite to each other may have things in common. The skill of recognizing similarities and differences is important. It helps you evaluate the value of ideas.

Reread the section of this case study that describes the roles of American women in the Vietnam War. It begins on page 85. There are some similarities between the roles that women played and the roles that men played. There are also some differences. To help you identify similarities and differences, copy the chart below on another piece of paper. Then complete it.

The Roles of American Women in Vietnam

Combat Roles

Facing Danger

Their Jobs

Answer these questions below your chart or on another piece of paper.

1. What are the similarities?

2. What are the differences?

3. In future wars, should there be any difference in the roles that men and women play? Explain your answer.

Panic-stricken Vietnamese refugees cling to a giant U.S. helicopter as it prepares to take off from the city of Xuan Loc in the last days of the Vietnam War.

THE FALL OF SOUTH VIETNAM

CRITICAL QUESTIONS

- Did the United States abandon South Vietnam when it signed the peace accords in January 1973?
- What happens to the losing side in a war when a city falls to its enemies?

TERMS TO KNOW

- evacuate
- anti-revolutionary
- embargo

ACTIVE LEARNING

After you read this case study, you will make a poster that advertises a television story about Vietnam. This story could be a documentary or a fictional account of the fall of South Vietnam. At a number of places in the case study, you will be asked to create a sketch for such a poster. You will then decide which sketches you will use in your finished poster.

, almost fully loaded, was waiting on
...way at the Saigon airport. A C130 is not
...ggest transport plane. However, it can still
...d hundreds of people. All night long,
...mericans and South Vietnamese had been
waiting to leave Vietnam. They clutched their
passports and a few personal belongings as they
entered the plane. Many of the Vietnamese cried.
They knew that they might never see their
homeland again.

The pilot, Air Force Captain Arthur
Mallano, looked out his cockpit window. He
saw what he thought was lightning in the sky.
He said to his co-pilot, "Gee, that thunderstorm
is getting closer. It's moving toward the field,
fast."

Mallano noticed that the flashes were not
just white, but many colors. They were red, blue,
and green. Mallano realized that they were
actually rockets. The North Vietnamese were
attacking the airport.

Bombs exploded all over the airfield.
Buildings, planes, and trucks burst into flames.
One of the first rockets exploded on a guard
house. It instantly killed two young Marine
guards, Darwin Judge and Charles McMahon.

Another early round hit a building in which
14 people were sleeping, most of whom were
high-ranking U.S. government officials. The blast
knocked them out of bed, but no one was hurt.

Another artillery round hit a gym with
1,500 South Vietnamese inside. The gym caught
fire, but a squad of firefighters was able to put
it out.

The crew of the C130 quickly boarded its
180 passengers. Another 80 people were already
lined up outside for the next plane. Mallano
realized that the situation was getting more
dangerous by the minute. He ordered, "Get the
last of them on. We're going!"

The plane rolled down the runway. Rockets
exploded around the plane. Mallano knew that
he had to get the plane in the air quickly. He
pushed the throttles as far back as he could. The
plane lumbered down the airstrip under its
heavy load. Finally, as it neared the end of the
runway, it rose into the air.

As Mallano looked down, he saw the whole
airfield. It was almost totally destroyed. South
Vietnam's last battle had begun.

1 The Beginning of the End

The wars in Vietnam lasted for 30 years. They
began when Vietnamese nationalists fought to
win independence from France. The wars briefly
ended on January 27, 1973, when American and
North Vietnamese officials signed a cease-fire.
This signing stopped the fighting.

By 1972, the war in Vietnam was very
unpopular in the United States. President Nixon,
a Republican, was running for a second term as
President. The Democrats nominated Senator
George McGovern of South Dakota. McGovern's
campaign message to the American public was
simple. He promised to end U.S. involvement in
Vietnam within the first minutes of his
Presidency. McGovern attracted the support of
many Americans who opposed the war. But
when it came time to vote, most Americans did
not support his position. Furthermore,
Americans were concerned about a number of
issues other than the Vietnam War. President
Nixon won reelection in November 1972 by a
wide margin.

The Spring Offensive

During the spring of 1972, the Communists
launched a new offensive on South Vietnam.
More than 120,000 North Vietnamese troops took
part in the attack. Their goal was to destroy the
South Vietnamese army and end the war. They
wanted to show the Americans that the policy
of "Vietnamization" would not work. The
Communists gambled that President Nixon
would not step up the war to oppose the new
offensive during an election year.

At the U.S. embassy on the morning of April 29, 1975, a long line of desperate Vietnamese snakes up staircases to the roof of the embassy. There, U.S. helicopters took as many refugees as they could carry to safety.

The North Vietnamese were wrong. Nixon responded by ordering heavier bombing of North Vietnam. U.S. planes bombed the northern port city of Haiphong for several days in a row. Other planes dropped floating bombs into the harbors of Haiphong and other North Vietnamese ports.

The Peace Talks

Talks to end the war had first been held in May 1968 in Paris, France. There was very little progress. The two sides could not even agree on the shape of the table to be used for the peace talks. The talks dragged on for years.

But these talks were just a cover for the real negotiations between the United States and North Vietnam. Starting in February 1970, two top officials, one American and the other North Vietnamese, were meeting in secret. On the U.S. side was Secretary of State Henry Kissinger. The North Vietnamese were represented by Le Duc Tho. Next to Ho Chi Minh, Le Duc Tho was the most important North Vietnamese official. For the next three years, these secret meetings helped lead to the withdrawal of American troops from Vietnam.

The Peace Accords

In 1972, the two governments reached an agreement. The most important terms of the agreement called for the following:

1. An in-place cease-fire. This term meant that after the fighting stopped, all Vietnamese soldiers would stay where they were. In other words, North Vietnamese soldiers would not have to leave South Vietnam.

2. The United States agreed to withdraw its remaining troops from Vietnam.

3. North Vietnam agreed to release 566 American prisoners of war.

On October 21, the North Vietnamese government approved the treaty. Henry Kissinger flew to Saigon to get South Vietnam's approval.

South Vietnam Rejects the Agreement

The South Vietnamese government would not accept the terms of the treaty. It was angry because it had not been told about the secret talks. The South Vietnamese were especially upset that the North Vietnamese troops would be allowed to stay in the south.

On October 26, North Vietnam and the United States announced that "peace is at hand." A week later, President Nixon won the 1972 Presidential election with 61 percent of the popular vote.

...ks Break Down

...vember 20, 1972, Kissinger and Le Duc ...met again. The United States changed its ...osition and insisted that the North Vietnamese agree to withdraw from the South. The North Vietnamese refused to accept this new condition. On December 13, the talks collapsed.

The Christmas Bombings

The United States had warned that if there was a breakdown in the talks, the United States would launch a new offensive, using massive military force against North Vietnam. One week before Christmas, U.S. aircraft bombed Haiphong, North Vietnam's main harbor, and Hanoi, its capital. The bombings continued for 11 days. It was the most intensive bombing campaign by the United States since World War II.

The bombings brought the North Vietnamese back to the peace talks. The next day, the U.S. and North Vietnamese governments again reached a settlement. The final settlement was the same one agreed to in October. The 150,000 North Vietnamese troops would remain in the South and the United States would withdraw all of its forces.

On March 29, 1973, the longest war in the history of the United States officially came to an end. On that day, North Vietnam released what it said were the final American POWs. The last few GIs boarded a flight for home. Only about a thousand U.S. government officials, Marines, and reporters remained in Saigon. Even though many thought that the war was over, they would find out that the Communists had not yet given up their cause to take over the entire country.

Jubilant Communist soldiers wave their flag on the grounds of the Presidential Palace in downtown Saigon. Earlier that day, they had crashed their Soviet-made tank through the palace gates, marking their victory over South Vietnam.

2 The Final Offensive

In the spring of 1975, two years after the signing of the Peace Accords, the Communists launched their final offensive against South Vietnam. In just three weeks, they captured a number of important South Vietnamese towns. The United States protested but did not act to protect the South Vietnamese.

The North Vietnamese kept pushing south. Two of South Vietnam's biggest cities, Hue and Da Nang, fell to the Communists. Within two weeks, the North Vietnamese had conquered half of South Vietnam. One-third of the South Vietnamese army was either killed or captured in the offensive. In Da Nang, the Communists captured more than a billion dollars worth of U.S. military supplies.

The sudden turn of events caused panic among the South Vietnamese. A flood of refugees fled south to escape North Vietnamese troops. They hoped to reach the coast and find boats that would take them out of Vietnam.

The migration of people from central areas in southern Vietnam to the coast is known as the "Convoy of Tears." A half-million people slowly trudged south along a narrow, winding road known as Highway 7. Military trucks pushed their way through the crowd. The refugees were constantly shelled by the North Vietnamese. Only one in four people made it to the coast. The rest either died or were captured by the Communists.

The Fall of Saigon

By April 9, 1975, the Communist forces had moved to within 40 miles of Saigon, the capital of South Vietnam. The town of Xuan Loc, just 38 miles from Saigon, was the key to victory for the North Vietnamese. If the Communists captured the town, then the road to Saigon would be clear.

The battle for Xuan Loc was fierce. About 5,000 South Vietnamese troops held off nearly 40,000 North Vietnamese for 12 days. But on April 21, the Communists took control of Xuan Loc.

The North Vietnamese troops had a clear path to controlling Saigon and to victory. South Vietnam's president resigned and left Vietnam in response to the defeat.

Active Learning: Imagine that you are a Vietnamese person who has worked closely with the Americans. What are you feeling as the South Vietnamese army seems to be losing the war? What concerns do you have about your family? Sketch out the words and pictures that you might use in the poster that advertises your television story.

he United States Leaves

Since the signing of the Peace Accords in Paris, the last American troops had pulled out of Vietnam. North Vietnam had returned 591 American prisoners of war.

But the war was not over. There were still about 1,100 Americans left in Vietnam. They included newspaper reporters, U.S. government officials, and several hundred Marines. There were also thousands of Vietnamese in Saigon who had loyally worked for the United States during the war. They had been promised that, if the United States pulled out of Vietnam, they and their families would not be left behind.

In the early morning of April 29, 1975, the people of Saigon awoke to the sound of artillery fire. Rockets were screaming into Tan Son Nhut Air Base near Saigon.

North Vietnamese pilots blasted the airport. All the runways were torn apart. Burning trucks and planes were everywhere.

A huge American fleet waited off the coast in the South China Sea to **evacuate**, or remove, the Americans. Because of the destruction of Ton Son Nhut Airport, fixed-wing airplanes could no longer be used. Helicopters would have to evacuate the people.

The airlift of Americans had already been planned. It was code-named "Operation Frequent Wind." The remaining Americans in South Vietnam had been given directions in case of an emergency evacuation. They had been told to gather on particular rooftops after they heard a special coded message on the U.S. Armed Forces Radio.

The special message was played at noon on April 29, 1975. It was in two parts. First came the announcement, "It is 105 degrees and rising." Then the radio played the song "I'm Dreaming of a White Christmas." The message was repeated every 15 minutes.

Americans in Saigon dropped everything. They had only a few hours to reach their designated rooftops and evacuate Vietnam.

Even though Operation Frequent Wind was planned long before April 29, there was a great deal of confusion. People gathered at the landing zones, but the helicopters didn't come. The panic grew.

Growing Desperation

In the weeks leading up to the fall of Saigon, thousands of South Vietnamese had tried to leave Vietnam. More than 100,000 had bought airplane tickets to other countries. With the destruction of the airport, however, no planes could take off or land.

Fear rose in the city. Thousands of Vietnamese tried to climb the walls and gates of the U.S. Embassy to get to safety. They hoped that the United States would protect them from the Communists if Saigon fell. Only 130 armed U.S. Marines prevented the embassy from being overrun.

People were desperate. One man shouted: "I'm Mr. Lon. I have served you for years. Please save me." The mob scenes in the streets made the evacuation difficult. Buses that were supposed to pick up Americans could not move through the jammed streets. An American reporter remembers the panic

We were scratching, clawing, pushing closer to the wall of the embassy. There was a pair of Marines on the wall. One of them looked down at me. "Help me," I pleaded. "Please help me." He reached down and pulled me up as if I were a helpless child.

Inside the embassy walls, the reporter joined more than 1,000 people who were waiting to be evacuated. Among these people were many worried South Vietnamese officials. Those officials included generals, the former mayor of Saigon, the police chief, and hundreds of embassy employees and their families.

Throughout the afternoon, large helicopters landed in the embassy parking lot. Americans and South Vietnamese scrambled aboard. The

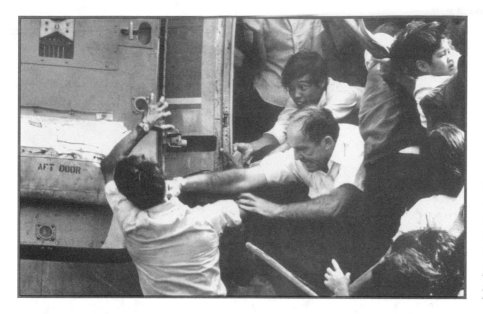

Desperate Vietnamese try to cram themselves into an already overloaded helicopter to escape advancing Communists. A U.S. official punches a man to free his grip on the helicopter's door.

helicopters kept landing about every ten minutes. Finally, at 4:20 A.M., the last helicopter took off from the parking lot. More than 400 Vietnamese were still left inside the embassy. Thousands more waited desperately outside the compound. They would be left behind.

The U.S. base in Saigon was now reduced to a few square feet on the embassy roof. The stairwell to the roof was crowded with people hoping to escape. Every few minutes, the helicopters landed. The embassy gate was opened a few minutes to let in a few more people. Sometimes, the Marine guards had to use force against people who tried to squeeze in. Finally, the embassy gate stayed closed. The Vietnamese who were recognized by Americans were lifted up over the wall. The guards knew that if they opened the gate again, they would never be able to shut it.

Ambassador Graham Martin was the last remaining U.S. government official in the embassy. At 4:30 A.M., he was still at his desk. He received his final order from the White House. It said

The President of the United States directs that Ambassador Martin comes out on this helicopter.

At 5 A.M., the ambassador boarded the next-to-last helicopter. The Vietnamese crowd begged not to be left behind. The last 11 Marines nervously waited on the embassy roof for the last helicopter. Below them, a riot broke out among the remaining South Vietnamese. The angry crowd set fire to cars. It unleashed its anger and frustration at being left behind. There was panic in the streets. A Vietnamese reporter recalls

You wouldn't believe what I saw in the streets. You could hear the bombs, the guns. Everyone running out in the street, shouting.

Just after 7:30 A.M. on April 30, 1975, the last helicopter landed on the embassy roof. The last Marine to scramble aboard carried the embassy's American flag. By noon, North Vietnamese forces controlled all of Saigon. The civil war in Vietnam was finally over.

Active Learning: Sketch out a poster on the last days of Saigon. What words and pictures will you use in your poster?

There were many heroes that final day. There were young embassy officers who risked to get their Vietnamese friends on helicopters. The helicopter pilots were [...] They just kept coming and coming. They [...] for 10 to 15 hours straight. The landing conditions were very difficult, especially after dark. At one point, an embassy official had all the embassy's cars parked around the landing zone with their headlights on, so that the helicopters could land safely.

Finally, there were the last two heroes, U.S. Marine Lance Corporal Darwin L. Judge and Corporal Charles McMahon Jr. Early on that last day, they had been killed by rocket fire at the airport. They were the last U.S. soldiers to die in Vietnam.

Thinking It Over

1. What was the secret message to Americans and Vietnamese that the evacuation had begun?
2. Why do you think that the U.S. ambassador stayed at the embassy until the last moment of the evacuation?

4 After the Battle

Not long after the last American helicopter lifted off, Communist forces took over Saigon. At 11 A.M., a single North Vietnamese tank crashed through the gate of Saigon's presidential palace. It was soon joined by many others. They formed a semicircle around the palace. A Communist soldier raced to the balcony of the palace. He raised the Vietcong flag in victory. The other soldiers cheered and shot their weapons in the air to celebrate their victory.

The Silent Sound of Peace

The Communist forces were orderly as they took control. There were no reported cases of theft by the victorious soldiers. The soldiers paid for everything that they took.

The Communists took over the radio station in the city. They began to broadcast orders to the people of Saigon. The first order officially changed the name of Saigon to Ho Chi Minh

The North Vietnamese and U.S. governments reached a peace agreement in 1973 that ended the fighting between the United States and North Vietnam. Signing are Le Duc Tho, for the North Vietnamese, and U.S. Secretary of State Henry Kissinger.

City. The new name honored the Communist leader of North Vietnam.

On May 7, 1975, there was a big victory parade. It came on the twenty-first anniversary of the defeat of the French at Dien Bien Phu. For the first time since the French sailed into Da Nang harbor in 1858, Vietnam was free of foreign soldiers.

People who had been a part of the old government of South Vietnam were rounded up by the Communists. Most of the one-and-a-half million supporters of the former Saigon government were forced to move. Many were moved from Saigon to small farm communities in the countryside.

The Dark Side of Peace

About 200,000 people were sent to "re-education camps." They were forced to do hard labor in the camps. Some of the people sent for re-education were senior officials and former military officers. Others were simply educated people, such as doctors, dentists, nurses, and teachers. Instead of using their skills to help rebuild the country, the Communists sent them to the countryside to grow rice.

Many people in the South feared a bloodbath. It's not clear how many people the Communists killed. Many of the victims were high-ranking South Vietnamese officers. One study estimates that at least 65,000 people were executed by the new government between 1975 and 1983. Some of the people sent to re-education camps were released after a few months. Some, however, were imprisoned for more than ten years.

"A Lonely Place"

After the Communists took over, there was widespread fear in Vietnam. The government discouraged the people from talking with foreigners. School children were urged to tell police if their parents were involved in any "**anti-revolutionary** activity." Anti-revolutionary activities included speaking out against the Communist government and fleeing the country. If parents were planning to flee, their children were told to report them. A young South Vietnamese woman told a reporter, "Distrust makes the city a lonely place."

The Boat People

After the Communist takeover, there were hard times in Vietnam. Many people owned small businesses. Their businesses were closed. Many South Vietnamese tried to flee the country. They boarded small ships and fishing boats to sail away from Vietnam. They were called "boat people."

Many of the boats were small and not intended for long trips. They were often crowded. There was little food or water onboard. Many boats overturned and many people drowned. Pirates captured some boats and murdered the refugees. Some of the boat people made it to safe havens, such as Hong Kong or Thailand. Yet even in these countries, many people were turned away, or their boats were towed back to sea.

A Good Book to Read

Goodbye, Vietnam, by Gloria Whelen. New York: Alfred Knopf, 1992.

This novel describes the life of a 13-year-old Vietnamese girl named Mai. She and her family decided to flee Vietnam in a small boat with many other refugees. The book describes the terrible suffering experienced by the Vietnamese boat people.

Just ahead of the advancing Communists, refugees flee South Vietnam on barges. Many Vietnamese made the perilous voyage hoping to reach Hong Kong, the Philippines, or another free land.

Relations with the United States

The United States broke off all relations with Vietnam after 1975. The U.S. government placed an **embargo** on trade with Vietnam. An embargo is a government order that bans all trade with another country.

Many Americans are still opposed to close relations with Vietnam. Even after 20 years, some Americans cannot recover from the war.

The Vietnamese government has a different attitude. Officials point out that Vietnam fought the French for many years before the United States became involved. But since the end of the fighting with France in 1954, France and Vietnam have enjoyed good relations.

In 1994, President Bill Clinton lifted the embargo against U.S. investment and trade with Vietnam. In January 1995, Clinton announced that each country would open a diplomatic office in the other's capital. This means that representatives of Vietnam will be in Washington

to help businesses interested in trading in or with Vietnam.

Thinking It Over

1. Describe the first days of peace in Saigon.
2. What has happened to relations between the United States and Vietnam in recent years?

Active Learning: Imagine that you are a store owner in Vietnam after the Communist takeover. You decide to try to leave the country. Sketch out a poster that describes a television program about your attempt to leave Vietnam.

Going to the Source

From "'Cultural Pollution' to Pop Culture"

The following excerpt from a recent magazine article describes popular music in Vietnam.

Western popular music was often heard in South Vietnam in the 1960s and 70s. Today, it is in style once more. Even older tunes seem fresh to the younger Vietnamese and stir their parents' memories of the past.

Until recently, the Vietnamese government called Western popular music "cultural pollution." Officials now often permit pop music concerts. They think such events help to rebuild the country and open its doors.

Ho Chi Minh City's Culture and Information Bureau promises to permit many kinds of popular music shows, "provided they don't violate regulations and Vietnamese cultural traditions."

With that official seal of approval, pop music tapes and compact disks are on sale on every street of the big cities and even in remote mountain towns. Original music is expensive. Tapes cost about 100,000 dongs ($10), and CDs 250,000 dongs ($25). Counterfeit items smuggled in from China or Hong Kong, however, cost only 6,000 dongs for a tape and 25,000 dongs for a CD. The government-owned radio and television stations now broadcast live pop music concerts carried by satellite.

In 1995, some of the current favorite tunes in Vietnam were "Bad," "We Are the World," Michael Jackson's "Thriller," Madonna's "Secret," "Hello," "Say You, Say Me," Lionel Richie's "Nothing Gonna Change My Love for You," Whitney Houston's "Missing You," and Stevie Wonder's "I Just Called to Say I Love You."

The favorite groups in Vietnam today are the Rolling Stones, Boyz II Men, Aerosmith, Nirvana, and the Pet Shop Boys.

Young Vietnamese like to watch the MTV channel. They are especially fond of rap music by groups like Public Enemy and Snoop Doggy Dogg, even if they can't understand the words.

From David Tran, *"'Cultural Pollution' to Pop Culture,"* (WorldWise, vol. 5, no. 8), p.11.

1. How much does an original CD cost in Vietnam?
2. Why are Communist officials allowing Western popular music in their country today?
3. What are the favorite musical groups in Vietnam today?

Case Study Review

Identifying Main Ideas

1. What was the difference between the two candidates' views on Vietnam in the U.S. Presidential election of 1972?

2. Why did President Nixon bomb Hanoi and Haiphong around Christmas time in 1972?

3. Why did a riot break out after the last U.S. helicopter took off from Saigon?

Working Together

Form a small group. Write dramatic headlines about the key events discussed in this case study. Make a bulletin board display of your headlines.

Active Learning

Creating a Poster Review the notes that you took and the sketches that you made as you read this case study. Select one scene and use it to determine what story you will tell. Give attention to both the drawing and the words that you will use in the poster. It does not matter if you are not an artist. The ideas that you express in the poster are what is most important. Those ideas should give a clear picture of your story and your point of view.

Lessons for Today

Based on what you have read about Vietnam, when do you think the United States should get involved in conflicts in other countries? Are there situations overseas that involve our national interests? How should the U.S. government decide when to get involved? Name the countries that the U.S. government is involved with today. Read newspaper and news magazine articles to find out about the arguments for getting involved and the arguments against getting involved in foreign disputes.

What Might You Have Done?

Imagine that you are a South Vietnamese citizen who has worked closely with the Americans. The Communists are attacking Saigon. There is no time to go back to your home to get your family. If you act now, you will be safely evacuated, but your family will be left behind. If you stay, you may be imprisoned or killed. What might you do? Write a short response that describes your decision. Describe the consequences of that decision and your feelings about it.

Contrasting Theories with Reality

The Communists in Vietnam came to power with ideals based on the writings of the philosophers Karl Marx and Friedrich Engels. In 1847, Marx and Engels listed measures that would go into effect when Communists gained control of a government. Here are some of them:

1. Private ownership of land, factories, and natural resources will be abolished.
2. Each member of society will give as much as he or she can for the sake of all the people in the society.
3. The Communist state will be a paradise for workers.

Now answer the questions below about Communist ideals:

1. What are some of the things that the Communists would eliminate or abolish?
2. Do you think that these ideals would attract many followers today?

The gap between the ideal world and the real world is huge. Here's how a writer describes the economic situation in Vietnam after the Communists took power:

At first, the Communists left the farmers and merchants of the South alone. The Communists did not want to make enemies of the South Vietnamese nor make the economy any worse. But in 1978, the government took over all privately owned businesses. It also tried to force small farmers to combine their land into large farms that they would own and operate together. This plan also failed. Many peasants grew only enough rice for themselves. They turned the extra rice into alcohol, which they could hide easily. In the 1980s, the government of Vietnam gave up its attempt to control the economy. After that, farm production went up. Today Vietnam again produces enough food to feed itself.

The Language of Thinking

An ideal is a statement of how we would like things to be. For some of us, an ideal of beauty is the way a Hollywood star looks. An ideal of democracy might be the ideas that inspired the U.S. Constitution.

There is always a gap between ideals and reality. For instance, Hollywood stars have warts, pimples, and bulges. We just don't see these things after the makeup artist, the lighting expert, and the film editors do their jobs.

Copy the table below on a separate sheet of paper. Fill it in by using the information you have learned in the case study.

As a class, discuss why there is a gap between the real and ideal world. What motivates most people? How do these motivations clash with Communist ideals? What are some American ideals? Is there also a gap between American ideals and reality?

Present in Today's Vietnam	Yes	No
1. There is no private ownership of land.		
2. All people get what they need (food, clothes, etc.).		
3. Each member of society gives as much as he or she can for the sake of all people in the society.		
4. The Communist state is a paradise for workers.		

After five years in a North Vietnamese POW camp, Sergeant Donald Rander returns home to the United States in 1973. Here, he is greeted by his wife.

SOLDIERS RETURN HOME

CRITICAL QUESTIONS

■ How do countries honor their war veterans?

■ What happens when veterans return home from fighting an unpopular war?

TERMS TO KNOW

■ military police (MP)

■ GI Bill

■ Post-Traumatic Stress Disorder (PTSD)

■ missing in action (MIA)

■ prisoner of war (POW)

ACTIVE LEARNING

After you read this case study, you will be asked to design a memorial to the men and women who served in Vietnam. You may choose to honor the soldiers or other service or support people by highlighting an act of courage or kindness. Or you might want your memorial to make a statement about the war in general. Think about a design for your memorial as you read this case study.

David McTamaney was returning home after his year of duty in Vietnam. He was proud of his service. For the first time, he wore some of the ribbons that he had earned. He was happy to be home.

He arrived at Oakland Air Force Base. As he left the plane, he noticed a crowd of about 200 people. They were standing by a fence. **Military police**, or MPs, were stationed in front of the crowd.

McTamaney couldn't make out what the crowd was saying. He moved closer. Suddenly, an egg landed at his feet. At first, he looked up in the air for a bird. Then he began to hear what the mob was shouting: "How many babies did you kill today?"

McTamaney suddenly realized what was happening. He had been warned not to expect any welcome-home committees, but he did not expect a hostile crowd.

He asked one of the MPs who these people were. As he did, a woman leaned back and spit

on him with all her strength. The MP told him just to ignore her.

On his way home to New York, he had to switch planes in Chicago. Walking through O'Hare Airport made him feel more uncomfortable than walking through the rice paddies of Vietnam. People pointed at him, laughed, and made comments. While he was in the airport waiting area, he offered his seat to an older woman. She looked at him and said, "I'd rather stand."

He grabbed his things and headed for the rest room. He thought that he might get out of his uniform. A young guy in the bathroom asked him if he had been in Vietnam. "Yeah," he said. "I just got back and I'm heading. . . ." He never got a chance to finish his sentence. The guy leaned back and spit in his face. McTamaney felt like ripping him to pieces, but let him go instead. McTamaney dragged his duffel bag into a toilet stall and locked the door. Then he put his face in his hands, and he broke down and cried.

1 Homecoming

In the past, veterans returning home from wars were honored as heroes and patriots. The veterans who returned from the two World Wars and Korea were greeted with parades by grateful civilians. They had fought in wars that most Americans supported.

For Vietnam veterans, it was very different. Much of the country did not support the war. For the first time, the United States seemed to have lost a war. There were no victory parades for returning soldiers. Instead, the veterans were made to feel as though they were to blame for America's defeat.

The American public treated many veterans with coldness. Some Americans took out their anti-war feelings on the veterans. One veteran said that people would come up to him and ask, "How does it feel to kill somebody?" The

Veterans of previous wars were welcomed home with parades and thanks. For many veterans of the Vietnam War, however, their return was as difficult as their tour of duty in Vietnam.

veteran told them, "It felt a lot better than if he had shot me."

Many veterans were disappointed by the welcome they received at home. One veteran said

I thought I'd get a lot of respect, because I'd done something for my country. I thought that people would react to what I'd done and say, "Hey, good job. Good work."

Friends and family were sometimes as cruel as strangers. Some of the veterans were called "suckers" by their friends for volunteering or for having allowed themselves to be drafted. One veteran recalls that a friend called him a coward because he did not resist the draft.

Another veteran remembers how opposed his sister was to the war. She advised him to go to Canada to avoid the draft. But he went into the service instead and was sent to Vietnam. "Then, when I got home," he said, "she refused to come and see me. She wouldn't have anything to do with me for months."

Many of the women who had served in Vietnam also had a difficult time adjusting when they returned home. Many suffered from depression. The skills that they had developed in the military were not recognized or respected in the civilian world. Few people who had not been in Vietnam understood how the war had affected the veterans.

Welcome Home

Not all returning Vietnam veterans were treated badly. Many veterans received warm welcomes from friends, family members, and even strangers. Glen Endress remembered what happened to him when he arrived home from the war around Christmas in 1968. Endress was in an airport, waiting for his plane when suddenly a voice behind him said, "Merry Christmas, Sarge." He turned around, thinking it was another GI. Instead, he saw a middle-aged man with a young boy. The man asked Endress what time his flight was leaving.

Suspicious, Endress asked why he wanted to know. The man said that he wanted to invite him to his home for Christmas dinner. Endress thanked him, but said he didn't want to take the chance of missing his flight.

The man wished him "Merry Christmas" again and started walking away. Glen called out to him and asked, "Why would you invite a perfect stranger to your house?" The man told Endress that his son had died in Vietnam that past year, and "we wanted a soldier at our table for Christmas dinner."

There are other stories of kindness toward returning veterans. There were cases in which taxi drivers refused to charge men in uniform for cab rides. Flight attendants offered some veterans first-class seats without extra charge.

Keith Brumbaugh, a Chicago veteran, did not need a parade. After his discharge, he became a student at Kent State University. In the late fall of 1970, his veterans group sponsored a weekend party for disabled veterans. That Saturday night, the group took the veterans to a basketball game. Many of the disabled veterans were in wheelchairs. Their chairs were lined up on the floor under one of the baskets. Before the game started, the announcer told the crowd about the veterans. The entire audience stood up and cheered for five minutes. (You read about anti-war demonstrations at Kent State in Case Study 5). Brumbaugh experienced his "parade" that weekend.

Thinking It Over

1. What were some of the differences between how Vietnam veterans were treated and how veterans of previous wars had been treated?

2. How did the treatment of the returning Vietnam veterans show the divided attitude of Americans toward the war?

It took years before the American public could accept Vietnam veterans as heroes. Here, in a 1968 ceremony, President Lyndon Johnson presents the Medal of Honor to Specialist 5 Dwight Johnson.

2 Adjusting to Life at Home

The vast majority of soldiers returning from Vietnam had little trouble going back to their old lives. About two-thirds of the veterans enrolled in universities and colleges under the **GI Bill**, a government program that pays educational costs for veterans. Many thousands of veterans would never have been able to go to college without the GI Bill.

A recent government study shows that most Vietnam veterans have done quite well adjusting to civilian life. The study included interviews with 15,000 veterans. Ninety percent said that they were working. The same percentage said that they were happy with their lives.

Some veterans have won personal and professional success since returning home. Rocky Bleier was badly wounded in the war. He was able to overcome his injuries and later became a star running back for the world champion Pittsburgh Steelers football team.

Many veterans started their own businesses. Others became executives of some of America's largest companies. Fourteen veterans have served in Congress. Several have been elected governors of their states.

Invisible Wounds

Some veterans, however, have had difficulty readjusting to civilian life. They had no visible wounds. Instead, the damage that they experienced was to their emotions. For some veterans, the difficulty in readjusting was temporary. They felt that sometimes people at home did not understand what they had been through in Vietnam. Many felt misunderstood when they came home. Another veteran said that he still carries around a lot of guilt—"guilt about being in Vietnam. Guilt about leaving the other guys. Guilt about surviving."

Pinkie Hauser remembered just wanting to be alone when she came home. (See Case Study 6.) Her mother would try to get her to talk. Her mother would ask, "Well, what was it like over there?"

"Mom, I just don't want to talk about it," Hauser answered.

Another veteran said that he slept on the floor during the first week that he was home. He said

I just couldn't get comfortable in a bed. I didn't know how to act, didn't know what kind of clothes to buy, didn't like anything.

A nurse recalled that she had been home for only a few hours when she started getting sick: "It was horrendous. I couldn't cry, but I had this terrible headache. Then I started throwing up. I threw up and threw up, and when it was over, I was OK. The headache went. The depression went."

Emotional Problems

Many Vietnam veterans suffered emotional problems upon their return. Some still have nightmares about the war. One ex-soldier explained, "I still dream about it. My wife hears me screaming in the middle of the night."

Many veterans are still troubled by memories of death and dying. Some dream of dying or being wounded in Vietnam. The memory of a friend dying haunts many veterans. One army veteran described the pain that he still feels

I would like to forget the screams I heard from the men who got shot. There is always a constant reminder that flashes you back right to them. Maybe the helicopters that go over, the police helicopters. It throws me right back into Vietnam. A noise, a big firecracker, a gun, a backfire. Anything that resembles somebody getting shot at.

Some veterans have been bothered by the suffering of Vietnamese civilians, especially children. One soldier said, "What really hurt was the civilians being killed. I still think about it. I wish I could forget, but I can't."

In the 1970s, psychologists gave a name to the emotional illness that some veterans were experiencing. They called it **Post-Traumatic Stress Disorder** (PTSD). This illness is similar to what was called "shell-shock" in World War I. During World War II, doctors said that victims were suffering from "battle fatigue."

One veteran described what PTSD feels like. He was out on a date and decided to see a film about Vietnam called *The Deer Hunter*. After a while, he forgot that he was in a movie theater. He thought that he was back in Vietnam. In one scene, the GIs are caught in a battle. The veteran said, "If I had had a gun on me, I would have started shooting." He said that he really came apart. He remembered

I crouched down behind the seat. I didn't know it was a movie anymore. I was back in the war and that was what I had to do.

A Good Movie to See

The Deer Hunter, directed by Michael Cimino. Universal Pictures/EMI Films, 1978.

This film is a realistic portrayal of the brutality of war and its effect on three young men. The three men are taken prisoner in a skirmish with the Vietcong. After brutal treatment, the Americans escape. The last part of the film deals with how each of the three adjusts to life after leaving the service.

Drug and Alcohol Abuse

There was widespread drug and alcohol abuse among the troops in Vietnam. In the mid-1970s, the Department of Defense released figures showing just how widespread these problems actually were. Between 1968 and 1972, about 30 percent of the soldiers in Vietnam used hard drugs, such as heroin. According to the Department of Defense, one out of every five men serving in Vietnam during 1970 was addicted to some drug during his tour of duty.

Many GIs used drugs and alcohol almost every day while in Vietnam. Some used drugs and alcohol to escape their fears and the horror of war. The Department of Defense study estimated that between five and ten percent of the veterans returned home with a drug or drinking problem. Nearly a third of the men in Veterans Administration hospitals today are there for treatment of alcohol-related problems.

The majority of Vietnam veterans, though, returned home without either a drug or an alcohol problem. It was a minority of soldiers who developed a substance-abuse problem.

Thinking It Over

1. What are some of the signs of Post-Traumatic Stress Disorder?
2. What are some of the lasting problems that some Vietnam veterans have faced?

3 The Healing

Since the 1970s, the attitude of the American public toward Vietnam veterans has changed. The war is still remembered as a time of great national pain. However, time has begun to heal the bitterness that many people have felt. By the late 1970s, the American people realized the sacrifices that the veterans had made for their country. A 1979 poll showed that twice as many Americans viewed Vietnam veterans as victims of the war rather than "warmongers," or people who enjoy war.

Veterans themselves have helped to change the public's perceptions of Vietnam veterans and the war. Some veterans speak at high schools and college campuses. They share their stories and discuss their feelings. These experiences have helped Americans understand the pain that the soldiers have undergone.

The Vietnam Veterans Memorial

Jan C. Scruggs was a young Vietnam veteran. He was sent to Vietnam in 1969 at the age of 19. He was wounded in combat and won a medal for bravery. After his year of duty in Vietnam, he returned home. Like other veterans, he wondered why little had been done to honor the men and women who had served in Vietnam.

In 1979, Scruggs decided to do something about the lack of recognition that Vietnam veterans had received from the public. He wanted to build a memorial. He was enthusiastic

Family, friends, and veterans visit the Vietnam Veterans War Memorial to honor the 58,000 Americans whose names are inscribed on the 400-foot-long memorial.

Going to the Source

A Mother Visits the Vietnam Veterans Memorial

Of the millions of people who visit the Vietnam Veterans Memorial every year, many visitors bring gifts to the wall, and leave letters. The letter below was left at the wall in 1983.

Dear Bill,

On this Memorial Day 1983, we come to this memorial to remember and we cry. We come to remember you and all the young men who died in Vietnam.

I and many others cannot understand the reason for it all but we must try to accept the fact that it did, indeed, happen. And all that we, the loved ones can do is to come here and remember, remember you as a baby, remember your first day of school, remember the love we shared and remember the day you died.

Oh, Bill, I miss you so much and the hurt never ends. You are still with us in our hearts and always will be.

I see your name on a black wall. A name I gave you as I held you so close after you were born, never dreaming of the too few years I was to have you. You may be gone, but you are not by any means forgotten. The love we shared will live on forever in my heart. You will always be my special love.

And as I look around at the thousands of other names, I remember that each name here represents, on the average, 20 years that each boy was some Momma's little boy, as you were mine. I miss you so.

Love,
Mom

From Sal Lopes, *The Wall* (New York: Collins, 1987), p. 65.

1. According to the letter, why did this mother come to the memorial?
2. How does she show that she sympathizes with all the other mothers who lost children?
3. How do you think that visiting the Wall could help relatives and friends of the people killed in Vietnam?

but lacked organizational experience. After a few weeks, he had collected just $144 toward building a veterans memorial. He shared his plan with two other men. The three started the Vietnam Veterans Memorial Fund.

They worked around the clock to find people who would donate money to help build a memorial. By the end of 1979, they had raised $9,000.

Choosing a Design

Scruggs and his friends had no idea what the memorial should look like. They decided to hold a design contest. People from across the country were invited to send in their ideas. More than 1,400 people entered the contest.

Finally, the three men chose the winning design. It was the work of a female college student named Maya Xing Lin. The Lin design called for a wall made out of two massive slabs of black granite. Each one would be 200 feet long. The wall would rise to a height of more than 10 feet before angling back into the ground on both sides. The names of all the Americans who lost their lives in Vietnam—close to 58,000 people—would be carved in the stone.

Active Learning: Think about what you want your memorial to represent. What feelings do you want viewers to have? Be prepared to explain why you chose the design that you did.

The Dedication

The completed Vietnam Veterans Memorial was dedicated on November 13, 1982. More than a quarter of a million people came to Washington, D.C., to attend the ceremony. A total of 150,000 veterans marched in a huge parade. The parade included many veterans in wheelchairs. Vietnam veterans had finally received the parade that the nation owed them.

There were a lot of tears that day. Tears were shed by parents who had lost sons or daughters, women who had lost husbands or boyfriends, men who had lost their military buddies, brothers and sisters who had lost siblings, and friends who had lost friends.

The tears were for the people whose names were on the wall. But there were tears for the living veterans, too. Tears were shed for veterans who had been gravely injured in the war. Tears were shed for veterans who were hooked on drugs, suffering from PTSD, or in constant pain.

Today more than a million people a year visit the memorial. They come to mourn and to remember. Some visitors whisper words of love for lost ones. Many leave flowers, flags, photos, and medals. Every visitor is deeply moved by the memorial.

The Vietnam Woman's Memorial

Diane Carlson Evans was a nurse who served in Vietnam. In 1982, she went to Washington, D.C., to see the Vietnam Veterans Memorial shortly before it was officially opened. Like many others, she cried at the wall as she remembered the many people whom she had seen die. After her visit, she said

> I felt so empty. I thought of all the women I had served with and what we went through. I was beginning to realize the country didn't even know we were there.

Evans began to think about organizing a memorial to the thousands of women who served in Vietnam. She sought the support of other veterans for the project. Only nine people attended the first meeting that she held to begin organizing the memorial. The group called itself the Vietnam Women's Memorial Project. Soon interest in the project grew.

Evans and her supporters traveled throughout the country to raise funds for the

After a 1973 ceremony, Diane Carlson, founder of the Women's Vietnam Memorial Project, greets other women veterans next to the newly unveiled statue. The statue shows three nurses tending a fallen soldier.

memorial. Everywhere they went, they spoke about the important roles that women played in Vietnam. They also worked with members of Congress. Finally, in late 1989, President George Bush signed a bill into law that called for the building of a statue honoring women Vietnam veterans on the grounds of the Vietnam Veterans Memorial.

A design by Glenna Goodacre was chosen for the women's memorial. Her design shows four figures. The first is a kneeling woman holding a helmet. Her face reflects the pain of war. Next to her is a nurse cradling a wounded soldier. The figure of an African American woman in military fatigues stands next to the nurse. She is touching the shoulder of the nurse who holds the injured soldier and she is looking toward the sky.

Thinking It Over

1. How have public attitudes about the Vietnam War changed?
2. How was the design chosen for the Vietnam Veterans Memorial?

Active Learning: Glenna Goodacre chose to show four figures in her memorial. Each figure symbolizes something about the war. What do you think each figure symbolizes? You might also choose to have figures that symbolize something that you want to express about the war or about the men and women who served in the war.

4 Missing in Action

One wound that refuses to heal is the fate of Americans who are listed as **missing in action,** known as MIAs, in Vietnam and in other Southeast Asian countries. There are still 2,211 Vietnam MIAs. When the Paris Peace Accords were signed in 1973, the United States published a list of the men and women who were listed as either MIAs or **prisoners of war** (POWs).

POWs are people who are captured by an enemy and then put into prison.

About 600 American prisoners were released under the terms of the treaty. The remaining names on the list are of soldiers, sailors, pilots, and civilians who disappeared during the Vietnam War. Most are probably dead. Many disappeared during air crashes or fierce artillery battles. They are listed as missing because their bodies have never been found. Until there is solid proof of their deaths, they will remain on the MIA list.

One example of the difficulties involved in dealing with MIAs occurred in 1972. An American gunship was hit after a mission over North Vietnam. The crew parachuted to safety. The 14 soldiers onboard didn't make it out. A rescue team found the remains of only one man. The other 13 soldiers are listed as MIAs. Also on the MIA list, but assumed dead, are 436 Air Force pilots who crashed at sea and were never found.

Seeking more information about loved ones missing in action in Vietnam, two protesters handcuff themselves to a gate as part of a demonstration in front of the White House in 1985.

How Many MIAs?

MIAs are also the men and women who vanished after being taken prisoner by the Vietcong and North Vietnamese army. They were definitely alive when they were captured. No one knows what happened to them. The case of Army Staff Sergeant Burt C. Small Jr., is one example. Small was wounded in the leg while on patrol. South Vietnamese soldiers watched as four North Vietnamese soldiers led the American away. The sergeant was not among the Americans exchanged after the Peace Accords. To this day, he has not been seen again.

There are many possible explanations for the missing men and women. They may still be held captive. They may have died in the dense jungle growth that covers much of Southeast Asia. Others may have chosen to start new lives in Southeast Asia.

Congress has investigated the possibility that MIAs are still alive in Southeast Asia twice since the end of the war. In the 1970s, a committee within the House of Representatives spent 15 months reviewing the files on MIAs. The committee traveled to Hanoi, the capital of North Vietnam, to talk with North Vietnamese leaders. In December 1976, after concluding their investigation, the committee found that "no Americans are being held alive as prisoners as a result of the war."

In October 1991, a Senate committee held another MIA investigation. It spent more than a year examining the MIA issue. More than 1,000 people were interviewed. In the end, the committee reported that it could not find any Americans who had been knowingly left behind in Southeast Asia.

Thinking It Over

1. What is the difference between MIAs and POWs?
2. Do you think that MIAs could still be alive? Explain your answer.

Case Study Review

Identifying Main Ideas

1. Why do you think that Vietnam veterans were not treated in the same way as veterans from previous wars?

2. How did some returning Vietnam veterans react to American society?

3. How was money raised to build the Vietnam Veterans Memorial?

4. What conclusions did the October 1991 Senate committee reach about MIAs in Southeast Asia?

Working Together

Form a small group. Find images about the Vietnam War in newspapers, magazines, and other sources. Photocopy them. Then create a collage of your photocopies. Show the various aspects of the war. Use your finished product to honor the Vietnam veterans in your community.

Active Learning

Designing a Memorial Review your ideas for your memorial. Revise your rough sketches. Present your ideas to the class. Explain any symbols that you have used. What purpose should the war memorial have? What feelings do you want viewers to experience?

Lessons for Today

The Vietnam War caused huge splits in American public opinion. The war was fiercely supported as well as fiercely opposed. The Vietnam Veterans Memorial helped to heal deep wounds in American society. Today other issues divide American society. Some of these issues include crime, abortion, and gun control. Discuss your position on these issues. Could you reach a compromise with people with whom you disagree strongly? How can explosive issues like these be resolved?

What Might You Have Done?

Vietnam veterans did not get a warm homecoming from many Americans. Imagine that you are opposed to the war, as many young people were. Do you think that the people who opposed the war treated the veterans appropriately? How do you think you might have treated the returning veterans?

CRITICAL THINKING

Examining Moral Responsibility for the Vietnam War

The Language of Thinking

Criteria are rules, or standards, used to make a judgment. For example, your criteria for a good friend might be someone who can make you laugh and who can help you with your homework. Your criteria may be different from someone else's.

Values are ideas or beliefs that you consider important. For example, some people may value friendship, while others may value talent. Still others may value money more than anything else. Different people have different values.

Throughout our lives, we evaluate behavior. We decide whether a certain action is good or bad, right or wrong. An action that we decide is good or right we consider to be a moral action. In judging whether an action is moral, we consider the following:

- What is good behavior?
- What is bad behavior?
- What is the right thing to do?
- What is the wrong thing to do?
- What circumstances are involved in the action?
- What are the rules or laws concerning the situation?

Opinions may differ about a certain behavior. Some people may think that a certain behavior is moral. Some may think that it is immoral, or not moral. Some may think that it is neither moral nor immoral.

Use your own ideas and the information that you have learned about the Vietnam War to have a class discussion about the questions below. Remember the rules of debate. Allow each person a turn. Listen carefully.

1. What kind of behavior should be allowed in war? Should people be allowed to steal or murder? Explain your answer.
2. What aspects of the Vietnam War were moral or immoral? Explain your answer.
3. What should a soldier do if he does not think that the orders given to him are morally right?
4. What should the consequences be for disobeying an order?
5. What would you do in a situation in which you knew something was wrong but were afraid to oppose it?

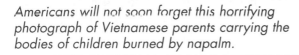

Americans will not soon forget this horrifying photograph of Vietnamese parents carrying the bodies of children burned by napalm.

THE LEGACY OF WAR

CRITICAL QUESTIONS

- How should the United States diplomatically deal with its former enemies?
- How did the Vietnam War change the United States?

TERMS TO KNOW

- *détente*
- recognize
- veto
- media
- oppressive

ACTIVE LEARNING

After you read this chapter, you will be asked to write an editorial on the impact of the Vietnam War on the United States. As you read, take notes to help you write the editorial. Remember that an editorial requires you to form an opinion and to take a single position.

Trinh was eight years old when her mother made the decision to leave Vietnam. Trinh's family lived in a small fishing village in an area that had been part of South Vietnam. When the war ended, the Communists came to Trinh's village. They closed her father's bicycle shop and sent him away to be "re-educated."

For several years, Trinh did not see her father. When Trinh was six, her father was finally released from the re-education camp. When he returned to his family, he was very ill. He died soon after he returned home.

Trinh's mother had thought about leaving Vietnam for a long time before she made up her mind. The night that Trinh and her mother began their journey out of Vietnam was very dark. They sneaked down to the river near their village. They were afraid and knew that if they were caught, the police would send them to prison. At one point along their journey, Trinh's mother bribed a guard with gold to keep him from arresting them.

The night was chilly. Trinh and her mother hid in the hold of a fishing boat, covered with tarps. The boat was uncomfortable and smelled of fish, but they were desperate to leave Vietnam to find a better life. They had to lie still as the boat passed several checkpoints. After many hours of waiting, the boat reached the open sea.

They sailed for days. Soon, there was no more food or water left. They hoped that they would be picked up by a ship from France, Britain, or the United States. But a ship from Taiwan was the first to stop the fishing boat and pick them up. They begged for food. The crew of the Taiwanese ship fed them and gave them water. Then they put Trinh and the others back on their boat. Three days later, an American ship picked them up and took them to Singapore.

While they were in Singapore, Trinh and her mother lived in a refugee camp. They lived in a house with many other refugees. Each family had a corner of a room to live in. They had a small gas stove for cooking. They ate only rice and noodles. They spent several months in the camp before they were able to go to the United States.

Trinh's older brother and sister had already emigrated to the United States, which helped Trinh and her mother get permission from the U.S. government to move to America. Finally, they took off for the United States. They spent a few nights in San Francisco while they were being checked for illness and disease.

Then came the big day. Trinh and her mother flew to Chicago to be reunited with the rest of their family. There were lots of tears when they finally saw each other, but they were tears of happiness. Trinh's family was together again.

After the Communist takeover, more than two million people fled South Vietnam, Laos, and Cambodia. The refugees shown here are on the deck of the aircraft carrier U.S.S. Midway in 1975.

1 A New Beginning

In the days and years that followed the end of the Vietnam War in 1975, thousands of people fled Vietnam. They left their country for many reasons. Some left because they had supported the South Vietnamese government and feared the new government. They were afraid of what might happen to them under Communist rule. Others left because of their religious beliefs. Many could not tolerate the idea of living in a Communist state. Still others left to escape the poverty of war-torn Vietnam.

More than two million people left the countries of Vietnam, Laos, and Cambodia. They all risked their lives to find happiness in other countries. All of the refugees were uprooted from their homes, friends, and culture. Most realized that they would probably never see their homeland again.

The Plight of the Boat People

Duy was 11 years old when he left Vietnam. Duy's father, like Trinh's father, had been sent to a "re-education" camp. He had been a professional architect in South Vietnam. While in the camp, though, he was forced to do hard labor in the fields for six years. Then he escaped with his family to the United States.

Duy's father now works in a restaurant. He is sometimes frustrated because he can't find work in the United States as an architect.

The Boat People

Many of the refugees, like Trinh, were boat people. They escaped by traveling in almost anything that floated. Some sailed to nearby places, such as Malaysia, Thailand, or Hong Kong. Others traveled thousands of miles.

The boat people needed courage and hope to survive their trips. Their journeys were often dangerous. One refugee who made the difficult voyage had been a captain in the South Vietnamese army during the war. When Saigon fell, he made his way to the coast, hoping to escape the country. The captain found a group of people trying to launch an open boat. It was an old fishing boat that had been abandoned. It was in very bad condition.

The captain helped push the boat into the water and then jumped in. There were 90 people onboard. Slowly, the boat floated southwest toward Malaysia.

The voyage took many weeks. There was little food or water for the refugees on the boat. Seven people died of starvation during the voyage. The captain feared that the waves would turn the boat over, drowning everyone. Only one man knew anything about sailing. The boat finally reached land. Today the captain works as an appliance repairman in California.

Many refugees, like the captain, made it to the United States, which welcomed nearly one million refugees from Vietnam, Cambodia, and Laos. From 1975 to 1986, about $5 billion in U.S. federal aid has been spent to help these refugees start a new life in the United States.

There are several reasons that the United States opened its doors to the Southeast Asian refugees. First, the United States has a long history of helping victims of war. Second, many of the refugees supported the American cause during the war. Third, the refugees opposed communism, and it was U.S. policy to help people escape life under Communist rule.

Nearly half of all the refugees settled in California. Many are quite successful. To get their new lives started in the United States, they took many different types of jobs. Many opened their own businesses.

Thinking It Over

1. Why did thousands of people flee Vietnam after the war ended?
2. What dangers did many of the refugees face?

Leaving on almost anything that could float, thousands of boat people risked the dangerous voyage across the South China Sea. These refugees were rescued from an open raft.

2 A New Vision of the World

The Vietnam War changed the United States in many ways. Opening the door to more than a million refugees from Southeast Asia was one way. The United States has also changed the way it deals with other countries.

The war taught Americans important lessons. One lesson was that having a strong military does not always ensure military victory. Although the United States had nuclear weapons, it could not use them. The United States also learned that it could lose a war.

Vietnam was a war fought by an "open society." Daily newspapers and television reports brought the violence and horror of the war into America's living rooms. Pictures of violence, burned villages, and maimed children bombarded Americans at their dinner tables. Unlike earlier wars, Americans at home were exposed for the first time to the realities of war.

The war in Vietnam changed Americans' attitudes about their role in the world, too. Since World War II, most Americans had favored an active role in world affairs. The Vietnam War made many Americans question the involvement of the United States in the internal affairs of other countries.

Many Americans concluded that the United States should not interfere in foreign countries unless it was necessary. Many believed that Americans should not be sent to die for causes that do not directly threaten the interests of the United States.

The Vietnam experience also forced Americans to look at U.S. foreign policy. It caused many Americans to see that the world had changed a lot since the end of World War II. One of President Johnson's closest foreign policy advisers was McGeorge Bundy. In 1978, Bundy said

We learned, in a very hard way that we had to understand our limitations.

Tensions Ease

The end of the Vietnam War caused an easing of the tensions between the United States and the Communist world. The French word *détente* is used to describe this new policy between the East and the West. After the United States pulled out of Vietnam, President Nixon attempted to improve U.S. relations with the two major Communist world powers—the Soviet Union and China.

In 1972, President Nixon flew to China to open communications. His visit paved the way for better relations. Eventually, the United States officially **recognized** the government of China for the first time since it became a Communist nation. To *recognize* a country means "to have official relations with it." However, it was not possible to improve relations with China until the United States withdrew from Vietnam.

Relations between the United States and the Soviet Union have also improved since the end of the Vietnam War. Both superpowers agreed to some control over their nuclear weapons. Several meetings between American and Soviet heads of government were held in the 1980s and 1990s. When the Soviet Union broke apart in 1990, the United States agreed to help Russia and the other countries that emerged from the split. Billions of dollars in U.S. aid went to the new nations. American businesses began investing in the new countries.

Thinking It Over

1. What does *détente* mean?
2. How did the Vietnam War affect the attitudes of Americans toward their country's role in the world?

3 Vietnam and Government Powers

In the United States, the Vietnam War represented, in a way, a contest between two of the branches of government: the President and Congress. They fought over the power to make war.

The U.S. Constitution gives both the executive branch (headed by the President) and the legislative branch (Congress) important powers. The President is commander in chief of the armed forces. But the Constitution says that only Congress can declare war.

Congress never declared war in Vietnam. President Johnson was able to send troops to Vietnam because Congress, in the Gulf of Tonkin Resolution, gave permission for him to use force. The longer the war went on, the more opposition to the war grew. Congress became more and more reluctant to spend billions of dollars on the war. Eventually, it voted to cut off all government spending for the war.

The War Powers Act of 1973

The framers of the U.S. Constitution expected the President and Congress to share responsibility for making war. The war in Vietnam caused many people to believe that the President had too much power. Congress acted in 1973 to limit the President's war-making powers. It passed the War Powers Act. This act limits the President's power to commit U.S. troops to combat. According to the act, the President can send troops into battle only if the United States, its territories or possessions, or its armed forces are attacked.

President Nixon vetoed the bill. The President has the power to **veto**, or reject, a bill. Nixon said that the War Powers Bill was dangerous to the best interests of the nation.

Congress, however, can still pass a bill that the President has vetoed. If the House of Representatives and the Senate can both get a two-thirds majority vote to support the bill, then it becomes law. To make the War Powers Bill law, Congress used this procedure and overrode the President's veto.

The Trust Factor

Before the Vietnam War, Americans had great faith in their government and their leaders. They trusted the President's judgment even if they did not always agree with him. Most people trusted that their leaders would take the right actions.

The Vietnam War was one reason that Americans began to question their trust in politicians. A top-secret Defense Department set of documents known as the Pentagon Papers revealed that President Johnson had made military decisions to increase American participation in the war. The decision to increase U.S. military involvement was made long before the President informed either the Congress or the American public.

Illegal actions that President Nixon took also increased America's distrust in its political leaders. Investigators uncovered evidence of illegal wiretaps and violations of election laws. These illegal actions became known as the Watergate scandal. In 1974, Nixon became the first President in U.S. history to resign.

The Role of the Media

The **media** also changed as a result of Vietnam. Media is a term used for radio, television, newspapers, magazines, and other forms of mass communication, whether print or electronic.

At the beginning of the Vietnam conflict, most people in the media supported the war effort. But over time, it became clear that there was a gap between what the government was saying to the public and what was really happening in Vietnam. Many news reporters thought that the American people were being lied to.

In the later years of the war, the media's reporting was very critical of the war. The media became a "watchdog" group for the public,

exposing problems in government or among elected officials. Today, as a result of the Vietnam experience, television and newspaper reporters often delve into every aspect of an issue, whether it deals with policy or the personal lives of elected officials. U.S. leaders are constantly being challenged. Their honesty is often questioned by the media and the public.

Thinking It Over

1. How did Congress try to limit the President's power to declare war?
2. What role did the Watergate scandal and Vietnam have in changing public attitude toward the U.S. government?

 The New Vietnam

For most young people in Vietnam today, the war is ancient history. Half the population of Vietnam is under 20 years of age. This means that these young people were not even born before the Vietnam War ended.

The world has changed a lot in the more than 20 years since the end of the Vietnam War. The Cold War between the Soviet Union and the United States ended. The Soviet Union collapsed. Third-World countries, such as India, Taiwan, Korea, and Thailand, now have booming economies. One-time allies of North Vietnam, such as China, are now seen as threats. The Vietnamese are worried about the power of China. In particular, they fear the growing Chinese influence in Cambodia and Laos.

Vietnam is still very poor, and it has many problems. But the country's leaders have recently introduced some reforms. The government no

Millions of Vietnamese, such as this boy who lost a leg during a U.S. bombing raid, will carry the scars of the war all their lives. Hundreds of thousands of Americans will also bear physical and mental scars.

We won, but I don't feel we have achieved our goals.

She admitted that the Communists have made many mistakes since the war ended. One mistake was treating the South Vietnamese like losers. She said that there were "too many re-education camps, too much punishment and not enough healing."

She is critical of the Communist leaders of Vietnam. She said that they are more interested in power than in the happiness of the people. Power, she believes, breeds corruption.

There is a lot of corruption in Vietnam today. Newspapers carry stories about government officials stealing from the public. Bribery is also very common. Hao believes that the tragedy of the war is the loss of values in the country. She said that all that the young people in Ho Chi Minh City today think about are motorcycles, television sets, fashions, and rock-and-roll.

Dr. Hao has little hope for change. She said

We are a nation that is still suffering. Our children are suffering.

She believes that the victory over South Vietnam was an empty victory. Unless prosperity is spread among all of Vietnam's people, "the revolution will have been for nothing," she said.

The Question of Human Rights

While Vietnam has made a lot of economic progress since the end of the war, it is one of the most **oppressive**, or cruel and unjust, nations on earth. Vietnam has a bad human rights record. Only one political party, the Communist Party, is permitted to participate in the government. People who disagree with the government are punished. Religious leaders face strict restraints on practicing their beliefs. People are often arrested and held for long periods of time without formal charges. The press has a limited amount of freedom to publish its stories.

Some Americans argue that U.S.–Vietnamese relations can improve only if the Vietnamese improve their human rights record.

longer completely controls the economy. People are allowed to own their own businesses again. Some land has even been returned to the peasant farmers.

Unhappy with Change

Dr. Duong Qunyh Hao was one of the founders of the Vietcong. She is a small, gray-haired woman now. But she was a tough fighter who spent more than eight years in the jungles of Vietnam during the war.

Looking back on the war, she is not happy. She said

The United States Recognizes Vietnam

Attitudes in the United States are still changing. In July 1995, President Clinton announced that the United States would restore full diplomatic relations with Vietnam.

Twenty Years of Change

The Vietnam of today is not the Vietnam that American helicopters left when they took off from the roof of the U. S. Embassy in April 1975. It is a new Vietnam. With a population of 70 million people, it is the second largest country in Southeast Asia. It is one of the most productive rice-growing areas of the world. It may hold important oil and mineral resources. Vietnam is also situated in an important position along the southern border of China.

American Business Returns

Vietnam is now eager to do business with the United States. It needs foreign money to build its economy. One Vietnamese official said

We are ready to close the chapter on the past and we are looking forward to a better future.

American businesses are also solidly behind better relations with Vietnam. They want relations to improve so that they can increase U.S. investment in Vietnam. Two U.S. oil companies are currently searching for oil in Vietnam. Automobile companies want to set up factories. U.S. banks already have branch offices in Vietnam.

On the outskirts of Ho Chi Minh City, a new model suburb is being built. A huge complex of homes, shops, a university, and a science park will replace the area where Vietcong guerrillas hid during the war. This complex was designed by an American architectural firm. When it is completed, it will provide jobs and homes for up to a million people.

Some Vietnamese Americans have returned to Vietnam to help the economy grow. Tony and Tim Nong left Vietnam at the ages of six and

A quarter century later, tempers have cooled, but many Americans still mourn men and women who were killed in the war. Here, visitors to the Vietnam Veterans Memorial remember a loved one.

seven. They grew up with an aunt in southern California. They now live and work in Vietnam. They operate one of Vietnam's most successful private tourist agencies with the help of their mother who never left the country. Called Ann's Travel, it now has five branches around the country. It is a symbol of the changes that are still occurring in U.S.–Vietnamese relations.

Thinking It Over

1. What reforms have been introduced in the new Vietnam?
2. What two issues have stood in the way of improving U.S.–Vietnamese relations?

Follow-Up Review

Identifying Main Ideas

1. Why was the United States eager to help refugees flee from Vietnam?
2. How did the Vietnam War affect the trust that Americans have in their elected officials?
3. Do you think that President Clinton was right in restoring full diplomatic relations with Vietnam? Explain your answer.

Working Together

Form a small group. Brainstorm on how the Vietnam War should be remembered. Ask yourselves how it affected the men and women who fought and the countries that were involved. What do you think will be the lasting effects of the war?

 Active Learning

Writing an Editorial Review the notes that you took as you read this chapter. Write a statement about how the Vietnam War should be viewed now that it has been over for more than 20 years. In the next two or three paragraphs, give details that support your statement. After writing your first draft, check it to make sure that it is clear and free of mistakes. Revise it and prepare a final copy.

Lessons for Today

The United States began to give aid to foreign countries in the 1940s. The goal at that time was to improve the quality of life for people living in countries that suffered damage during World War II. Today many people in the United States oppose giving foreign aid. What are some of the "pros" and "cons" of foreign aid? Do you think that Vietnam should be a special case?

What Might You Have Done?

Imagine that you are an American Vietnam veteran. Your army unit is planning a reunion. It will be returning to Vietnam. A visit is planned with several North Vietnamese soldiers who fought against the Americans during the war. Do you think that you might want to go? What feelings do you think you might have if you were back in Vietnam? What might you say to the Vietnamese veterans?

GLOSSARY

A

anti-revolutionary someone who opposes a revolution. After the Communists took over South Vietnam, they imprisoned anyone who spoke out against the new Communist government or tried to flee the country. They viewed these activities as anti-revolutionary.

B

battle fatigue the emotional illness that some Vietnam veterans experienced

C

cease-fire a short pause when opposing sides in a conflict agree not to fight

coalition an alliance of nations

Cold War a conflict between the United States and the Soviet Union and their allies in which both sides built up their military forces and weapons but avoided a major "hot" war with each other.

commons a large, open area in the center of a town or campus

corrupt dishonest

curfew an order to be home during certain hours

D

defer to excuse someone; in the Vietnam War, to excuse someone from the draft

détente an easing of tensions between countries

draftee someone who is ordered by the government to enter the armed forces

E

embargo a government order that bans trade

enlistee someone who volunteers to serve in the military

escalate to increase

evacuate to remove or leave an area

G

generation gap the differences in attitudes or opinions between one generation and another

Geneva Accords the peace treaty that ended the first Vietnam War (1946–1954)

GI Bill a government program that pays the educational costs for veterans

Green Berets members of the Army Special Forces who were sent to train and advise the South Vietnamese army

grunts infantry or ground soldiers

guerrilla warfare a kind of fighting in which small groups of soldiers make surprise attacks against government soldiers and enemy buildings and bases

H

hamlet a small village

I

immunity the government agrees not to punish a person for what he or she did, even if the person is guilty of a crime

incursion a raid in which soldiers enter, then quickly leave, a country

interpreter someone who translates one language into another language

L

legacy something that one generation leaves to another

M

media radio, television, newspapers, magazines, and other forms of mass communication

military police (MP) soldiers who carry out police duties in the armed forces

missing in action (MIA) military and support people who have not been accounted for

N

nationalize a government takeover of private land or industries

negotiations discussions whose purpose is to form an agreement

neutral not taking a side in a conflict

O

oppressive harsh

P

parallel an imaginary east–west line on a map that shows a precise location

populous a nation that has many people

prisoner of war (POW) someone who was captured by the enemy during a war

psychological victory a victory that is more important for its effect on people's minds than for its military significance

R

recognize to have official relations with a nation

reinforcements troops sent to help soldiers who are already under fire

repel fight off

Reserve Officers Training Corps (ROTC)
a program that trains students for the military

resolution a formal statement made by a group

retaliate to pay back an injury with another injury

S

sanctuary a safe place that can not be attacked

search and destroy an intensive scouring of an area to kill all enemy troops there

self-sufficient a term that describes people who are able to provide for themselves

sonar a device that picks up sound bounced off an object in water

symbol a picture that stands for another object or person

T

traitor a person who is disloyal to or betrays his or her country

U

unanimously without opposition

unify to bring together

V

veto the power of the President to reject a bill that Congress has passed

volunteer in the military, someone who agrees to join the armed forces without being drafted

INDEX

M

Maddox, U.S.S., *13*, *20*
Mao Zedong, *8*
Martin, Graham, *95*
Marx, Karl, *101*
McCarthy, Eugene, *34*
McGovern, George, *90*
McNamara, Robert, *19*
Medina, Ernest, *40*, *42–43*, *45*, *48*
Missing in action (MIAs), *111–112*
Morse, Wayne, *17*, *19*
My Lai Massacre, *11*, *39–50*

N

National Guard, in Kent State shootings, *68*, *69*, *71–72*, *73*
National Liberation Front. *See* Vietcong
Nixon, Richard, *11*, *46*, *48*, *119*
    bombing of Cambodia, *54*, *55*, *56*
    bombing of North Vietnam, *91*
    and Congress, *58–59*
    election of 1972, *90*, *91*
    invasion of Cambodia, *52*, *55–56*, *58–59*, *64*
    on Kent State shootings, *72*
    Vietnam policy of, *53–54*, *73*, *90*
    Watergate scandal, *120*
North Vietnam
    bombing of, *15*, *18*, *35*, *91*, *92*
    formation of, *9*
    peace agreement with, *35*, *91*, *92*, *96*, *112*

O

Operation Frequent Wind, *94*
Operation Menu, *54*

P

Parrot's Beak offensive, *56*
Peace Accords, *35*, *91*, *92*, *96*, *112*
Pearl Harbor, attack on, *65*
Pentagon Papers, *120*
Phnom Penh, *57*, *58*
Post-traumatic stress disorder (PTSD), *107*
Prisoners of war (POWs), *16*, *22*, *82*, *92*, *111*

Propaganda, political, *24–25*
Pro-war demonstrations, *66*
Psychological victory, *29*, *38*

Q

Quang Ngai province, *40*

R

Race relations, *84*
Refugees, *89*, *90*
    boat people, *97–98*, *116–117*, *118*
    in Cambodia, *57*
    Convoy of Tears, *93*
    in embassy airlift, *91*, *94–96*
Reserve Officer Training Corps (ROTC), *65*, *69*, *72*
Rhodes, James, *70*
Ridenhour, Ron, *46*
Rusk, Dean, *19*

S

Saigon
    attack on U.S. embassy, *27–28*
    evacuation of U.S. embassy, *94–96*
    fall of, *93*, *97*
Scruggs, Jan C., *108*, *110*
17th parallel, *8*
South Vietnam
    corruption in, *10*, *65*
    Diem regime in, *10*
    fall of, *93–97*
    formation of, *8–9*
    U.S. withdrawal from, *94–96*
    See also Refugees
Soviet Union, *8*, *119*, *120*
Special Forces. *See* Green Berets
Spring Offensive, *90*

T

Tet Offensive, *11*, *28–32*, *37*, *38*
Thailand, *10*, *21*, *56*
Thompson, Hugh, *45*, *46*
Ton Son Nhut Airport, *94*

V

Veterans, *103–114*
Veto, *119–120*

Vietcong, *10*, *20*, *80–81*
    account of Mai Lai massacre, *45–46*
    in Cambodia, *52–54*, *57*
    in Quang Ngai province, *40*, *42*
Viet Minh, *11*
Vietnam
    Communist takeover of, *97–98*
    division of, *8–9*
    economy of, *101*, *120–122*
    human rights in, *122*
    independence from France, *8*, *90*
    U.S. relations with, *98*, *121–122*
    See also South Vietnam; North Vietnam
Vietnamization policy, *73*, *90*
Vietnam Veterans Memorial, *108–111*

W

War Powers Act of 1973, *119–120*
Watergate scandal, *120*
Westmoreland, William, *31*, *32*, *38*, *45*, *47*
Women's Vietnam Memorial Project, *110–111*
Women in Vietnam, *78*, *83*, *85–86*, *105*
World War I, *85*
World War II, *7*, *8*, *65*, *82*

ACKNOWLEDGMENTS

Grateful acknowledgment is made to the following publishers, authors, and other copyright holders:

p. 18: From *Then the Americans Came* by Martha Hess. New York: Four Walls Eight Windows, 1993. Reprinted by permission of the publisher.

p. 33: From *Dear America: Letters Home From Vietnam* edited by Bernard Edelman. New York: Norton, 1985. Reprinted by permission of the author, Fred Downs Jr.

p. 57: From "Cambodia: A Reporter's Diary" by Arnaud de Borchgrave. *Newsweek*, June 15, 1970. Reprinted by permission of the author.

p. 70: From *The Kent State Coverup* by Joseph Kelner. New York: Harper, 1980. Reprinted by permission of the author.

p. 83: From *To Those Who Have Gone Home Tired* by W.D. Ehrhart. New York: Thunder's Mouth Press, 1984. Reprinted by permission of the author.

p. 109: From *The Wall* by Sal Lopes. New York: Collins, 1987. Reprinted by permission of the author.

Globe Fearon Educational Publisher has executed a reasonable and concerted effort to contact the following authors: Brian Sullivan, for his letter printed on page 41, and David Tran, for his article printed on page 99, "From 'Cultural Pollution' to Pop Culture," published in *WorldWise* magazine. Globe Fearon Educational Publisher eagerly invites any persons knowledgeable about the whereabouts of the authors or agents to contact Globe Fearon Educational Publisher to arrange for the customary publishing transactions.

Grateful acknowledgment is made to the following photographers:

Photo Credits: **Cover:** UPI/Bettmann; inset: Black Star; **p. 5:** UPI/Bettmann; **p. 6:** UPI/Bettmann; **p. 11:** UPI/Bettmann; **p. 12:** UPI/Bettmann; **p. 13:** AP Wide World; **p. 14:** UPI/Bettmann; **p. 17:** James H. Pickerell, Black Star; **p. 19:** UPI/Bettmann; **p. 21:** UPI/Bettmann; **p. 26:** UPI/Bettmann; **p. 28:** Wide World; **p. 29:** UPI/Bettmann; **p. 30:** National Archives; **p. 32:** UPI/Bettmann; **p. 35:** UPI/Bettmann; **p. 39:** UPI/Bettmann; **p. 40:** UPI/Bettmann; **p. 43:** UPI/Bettmann Newsphotos; **p. 44:** UPI/Bettmann; **p. 46:** UPI/Bettmann; **p. 47:** UPI/Bettmann; **p. 51:** James Pickerell, Black Star; **p. 53:** National Archives; **p. 55:** UPI/Bettmann; **p. 59:** UPI/Bettmann; **p. 63:** UPI/Bettmann; **p. 64:** UPI/Bettmann; **p. 66:** UPI/Bettmann; **p. 68:** UPI/Bettmann; **p. 71:** UPI/Bettmann; **p. 73:** UPI/Bettmann; **p. 77:** UPI/Bettmann; **p. 78:** UPI/Bettmann; **p. 80:** UPI/Bettmann; **p. 84:** Andrew Schneider, Black Star; **p. 86:** UPI/Bettmann; **p. 89:** UPI/Bettmann; **p. 91:** UPI/Bettmann; **p. 92:** UPI/Bettmann; **p. 95:** UPI/Bettmann; **p. 96:** UPI/Bettmann; **p. 98:** UPI/Bettmann; **p. 103:** UPI/Bettmann; **p. 104:** UPI/Bettmann; **p. 106:** UPI/Bettmann; **p. 108:** UPI/Bettmann; **p. 110:** UPI/Bettmann; **p. 112:** UPI/Bettmann; **p. 115:** UPI/Bettmann; **p. 116:** National Archives; **p. 118:** UPI/Bettmann; **p. 121:** UPI/Bettmann; **p. 122:** Bettmann